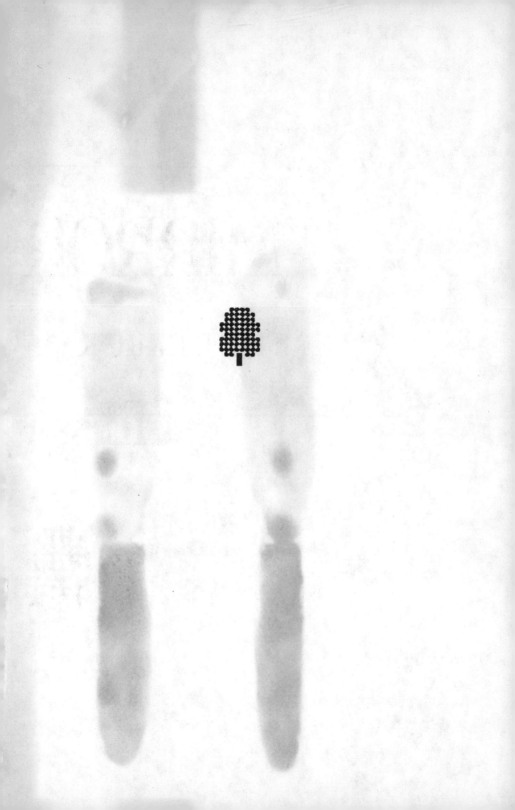

MIRROR

THE TERROR OF

Elissa

MIRROR

NOT BEING YOUNG

Melamed, Ph.D.

LINDEN PRESS/SIMON & SCHUSTER
New York

Published by Linden Press / Simon & Schuster
A Simon & Schuster Division of Gulf & Western Corporation
Simon & Schuster Building
Rockefeller Center
1230 Avenue of the Americas
New York, New York 10020
LINDEN PRESS / SIMON & SCHUSTER and colophon are trademarks of Simon
& Schuster
Designed by Eve Metz
Manufactured in the United States of America

10 9 8 7 6 5 4 3 2 1

Library of Congress Cataloging in Publication Data
Melamed, Elissa, date.
    Mirror, mirror.

    Bibliography: p.
    1. Women—Psychology. 2. Aging. 3. Middle-aged women. I. Title.
HQ1206.M396 1983   305.4′2   82-25869
ISBN 0-671-43429-2

Excerpt from *Jane Fonda's Workout Book* by Jane Fonda, copyright © 1981
by The Workout, Inc., used by permission of Simon & Schuster.
Epigraph from *Staying Hard* by Charles Gaines, copyright © 1980, used by
permission of Kenan Press/Simon & Schuster.

FOR ANNA RUBEE ISAACSON
    MY MOTHER

WITHDRAWN

Contents

THE DARK SIDE OF THE MOON

If woman is the moon, the second half of a woman's life is like the dark side of the moon. It is the side facing away from the world, man's world, and is therefore the half that is unknown, invisible, and often ignored. It can be the dark and difficult side of life for many women on whom the sun shined in their youth. If the moon were truly a woman, she herself would find her dark side mysterious, since she receives no reflection of it in the eyes of the world. Yet it is fully half her being whose presence she always senses.

The moon is a body—a heavenly body. Without her dark side she is one-dimensional, weightless: a paper cutout in the sky, the subject of romantic cliché. Her dark side gives her depth and mass. It is only through her body that the moon can come to know herself.

I got my first glimpse of the dark side of the moon fifteen years ago in a suburban beauty salon—the kind that serves bad champagne in the waiting room. A woman of about sixty came over to talk to Aldo, who was cutting my hair. On her head was an unnervingly uniform brown mass that seemed exempt from all laws of motion, and her skin was plastered with a tannish coating, further overlaid with spots of pinkish color. Only her eyeballs and the inside of her mouth were recognizably human tissue. She tilted her head a bit and asked querulously, "Aldo, do you think this makeup does anything for me? James just did it but I really trust your opinion and I want to know what *you* think."

I had a momentary vision of Aldo saying something like, "Good God, lady, who do you think you're fooling? Why don't you wash your face, put your hair back in a bun, never come here again and you'd look 100 percent better." Aldo of course merely made a comment such as "You really look fine, Mrs. Miller, but perhaps the base coat is just a bit too thick."

I knew then I would never go back to a place like that, without understanding or wanting to confront the complicated feelings the incident had raised in me.

As I look back, I am not proud of what I felt: a mixture of pity, scorn, and above all, denial that Mrs. Miller could have anything to do with me. Why was she so dependent on the hairdresser's opinion, for God's sake? Why couldn't she *see* herself? And I told myself loudly that this could never happen to me. After all, I was young! and life was still a fairy tale in which younger and older women were frozen forever as separate characters. (Of course, I was—I had always been—Snow White.)

I dismissed the incident, but I never forgot it. I must have filed it for future reference under "Distant Early Warnings," knowing dimly that I too would age someday—impossible as that seemed!

Yet one day, the memory of Mrs. Miller came back to haunt me. Somehow or other, I too was now over forty. I didn't really like it—even worse, I was ashamed to admit that I really didn't like it. I remembered my attitude toward Mrs. Miller and other women who clung to faded youth. Could this be me, looking uneasily in the mirror, wondering if a little Loving Care would be a good idea? I who was Snow White had turned into the stepmother! How had this happened?

After all, I was not a movie star who depended on youth for my livelihood. I was in good shape, not menopausal, and I enjoyed my life in New Mexico and my work as a teacher and psychotherapist. I was married to a man I loved and my three teenage children still talked to me. In short, I had nothing to complain about.

Besides, none of my friends said anything about such feelings, and the bookstores seemed to be full of books with titles like "The Prime of Your Life: The Book that Makes Old Age Obsolete" and "The Wonderful Crisis of Middle Age." They only made me feel more ashamed and did not explain the *persistence* of my uneasy feelings. My rational mind kept asking: "Why? What earthly difference does it make if I have a few wrinkles and gray hairs?"

As a psychotherapist, I realized that I was obviously dealing with something deeper than some wrinkles and gray hairs. I was feeling divided, divided against myself: a changeless person trapped inside a changing body; a centered person at odds with a needy person; an honest person ashamed of the "me" who wanted to play the youth game. A voice echoed in my head: "No, you are no longer the fairest in the land." All this was very unsettling, but also interesting! My vision turned inward, searching for the origins of my "stepmother syndrome." As I watched the reruns on my inner screen, certain scenes stood out:

Myself, age three, staring stupidly at my Mary Janes while Daddy's friends ask me, "Where'd you get those big blue eyes?"

Myself, at seven, being appraised at the dancing school and keeping my back turned to the wall: "Turn around, Elissa!" Hmmmmmmm . . . nice little head."

At age nine, hearing the story about my birth from Mommy: "I held back until after midnight so that you could be born on your father's birthday." She and I locked together in pain so that I could be born a birthday present for my father.

Then more inner movies of Daddy's little present, looking cute and dancing for the grownups. Starting to enjoy it now, perfecting my performing skills until I could get Those Looks whenever I wanted (oh, the power of it!).

Then, on to teenage triumphs, understanding exactly which images could be subtly shaped to earn my reward (their looks at my "great looks"). My marvelous antennae could sense the exact calibration of personal projection that would turn the heads: no difference now between a dance theater or a university dining hall; every entrance was a stage entrance and every doorway a pro-

scenium arch. I had elevated "looking presentable"—the minimum requirement for any woman—to the status of an art form: "having presence." Reveling in it now, one of the elect: a woman winning the only real game in town, and with an air of such perfect naturalness! My antennae were so sensitive that I knew I needed no makeup and could even pretend that I was not playing the game. I almost fooled myself.

And underlying it all, the classic Snow White story: Daddy's girl beating out Mommy.

My gut reaction to this private screening was: "I have been fooled—and foolish." I who had seen myself as a winner now felt as if I were waking up from a forty-year-long seduction. While I was young, because I was young, I had naïvely confused recognition of my youth and beauty with recognition of me. I had, in fact, identified the "me" with this frozen young personage. Like Sleeping Beauty, I had fallen into a trance around the age of fifteen from which I was just beginning to wake. It was becoming painfully clear that I had spent my life perfecting the game of pleasing and attracting others (particularly men) and relying on my youth and looks to do this much more than I had realized or cared to admit. I felt a bit like the addict whose bluff that "he can quit anytime" has just been called when the stuff is not available and he gets shaky. Now I knew what my "stepmother syndrome" was: withdrawal pains.

Yet, in spite of my shakes, I knew it was good to be finally waking up. I felt alive and full of questions: First, if the real "me" was not the same as this charming but static young person, then who was she? How could I discover her? And what were other women my age experiencing? I wanted to know how I was different from—and similar to—others.

I suspected that my involvement with "looks" had been greater than average; it had even shaped my professional choices: dancer, teacher. And even as a psychotherapist, I concentrated on the importance of posture, gesture, and movement. Nevertheless, I knew I could not be alone in my craziness: the multi-billion-dollar-a-year beauty industry reassured me of that. In a sense, every woman is a performing artist. I hungered for a perspective broader than my own personal history, for comrades in struggle, and for role models: women who had made peace with aging. What better way to get what I needed than to research the subject? I thought.

My early explorations were tentative. I simply began talking to women, asking them how they felt about aging. These first investigations confused me. Most of the women I talked to deprecated the youth game and minimized the amount of time, money, and effort they spent playing it. It seemed as if everyone *but* the woman I happened to be talking to was buying the Oil of Olay and Loving Care. And then I realized that possibly other women felt as I had: ambivalent about aging, but afraid or ashamed to say so.

I decided to confess to my interviewees that I had been having mixed feelings about aging myself that were hard to admit. The response to my candor was interesting. Immediately no one was neutral. Concern over aging was passionately denied (sincerely? defensively?) or it prompted outpourings of acknowledgment, confusion, resentment, and fear. But always, women's eyes would light up when they heard that I was investigating the subject of aging.

It gradually became clear to me that even in this liberated age, to "tell it like it is" about the youth game is to break a taboo. Our collective youth hangup was the Dirty Little Secret—the one aspect of aging we did not want to talk about.

For me, this work of self-confrontation and sharing was profoundly healing. I realized that I had created my own personal consciousness-raising process. Communicating it to others and making it a mutual exchange seemed like the natural next step.

One morning in 1978, sitting at home in the New Mexico sunshine, I decided to take that step—to create a consciousness-raising group for women over forty, a place where we could let all our age hangups show and, we hoped, re-envision the second half of life.

As with many pioneer efforts, we were given space in a sympathetic church, which used the adjoining chapel for wedding rehearsals. This situation contributed a moment of perfect irony. As our group assembled for the first time, the strains of the "Wedding March" wafted through the chapel doors. We looked at one another, caught between laughter and tears. There we all were, in various stages of marital harmony, disharmony, or singleness, coming together because the "Wedding March" had not led us to the "happily ever after" we had been given to expect. A better icebreaker could not have been planned.

Confessing to our youth hangups made me aware of how "fixated" we had become. Until we began to deal with the Peter Pan in ourselves, we had no idea how much we had arrested our development. When Freud talked about fixation, he was referring to the way people get stuck at certain points in their psychosexual development, preventing full maturation. It was clear to me that women have a "social fixation" on youth and young adulthood, which prevents their full maturation into the second half of their lives. This fixation is of such epidemic proportions that we accept it as normal.

And so we talked and measured this impact on our lives. We were no longer wistful thirty-five-year-olds in various stages of decay, but human beings who were looking foward, with all the hopefulness that implies.

However, new obstacles appeared as our work continued. We became aware that the root causes of our problems were only partially in ourselves. No matter how ready we were to move forward in our lives, there wasn't very far to go. There simply were not enough well-paying jobs, interesting roles, or available partners for older women. In such an unsupportive environment, how could we grow to our full stature?

As I began to probe this question, others presented themselves. I had begun my investigations in Santa Fe, a city of three cultures—Spanish, Indian, and "Anglo"—and had seen that aging was affected by culture. I wondered how women in other countries, not immersed in the youth culture of America, were dealing with aging. An opportunity to work in Paris gave me the chance to travel through Europe and continue my interviewing.

This turned out to be easy. Since I was not attempting to do a formal study, I simply "followed my nose," letting it lead me toward a deeper understanding of women's lives. I met women everywhere as I traveled, and talked to them and to their friends and neighbors. They were amazingly cooperative and as honest as they knew how to be. I developed a questionnaire which I felt free to modify as the need arose; it is included in the appendix.

I drank tea in Irish kitchens and champagne in Louis XV drawing rooms. I talked to academics, actresses, farm wives, prostitutes, jet-setters, housecleaners, lesbians, nuns, and others; I talked to over two hundred women in seven countries (France, Belgium, Ireland, England, Italy, Switzerland, and the United States).

If I had ever thought that this was solely an American problem, that idea was quickly dispelled. Even among the French (who do make more room for older women of special charm), the problem existed. It goes with urban living and the breakdown of traditional life styles more than with nationality. A Parisian secretary will be more concerned about aging than will a Minnesota farm wife. But it was nevertheless especially virulent among Americans. Even college-age women were affected (my youngest informant was twenty-one and my oldest, ninety-four).

As the book took shape in my mind, I also felt the need to talk to various experts such as physicians, psychologists, and anthropologists. And I also questioned my male friends about their relation to aging.

My feelings about doing the interviews were mixed. On the one hand, there was the pleasure of discovering that older women were for the most part likable and interesting—and often wise as well. I felt a bit like a lucky prospector finding gold nuggets wherever I went. But I also became acutely aware of the discrepancy between our strengths and our minimal opportunities to use them . . . as well as the damning fact that most of us accept these limitations as normal.

I sometimes saw us as beautiful, mature trees in a tiny greenhouse, pushing against the glass and getting bent out of shape in the process.

I began writing in Paris, in the winter of 1980. The peaceful

Sangre de Cristo Mountains I saw from my window at home seemed light-years away. My window on the world was now French television, bombarding me nightly with horror, violence—and men. Iranian men shaking their fists at me. Carter and Khomeini having their showdown. Cambodians dying because of a megalomaniac dictator. Our species seemed to have run amok, *and where were the women?* This question seemed somehow related to the greenhouse I had envisioned.

Suddenly the light dawned. I had been raised to suppose that men knew what they were doing. Could it be that in spite of their impressive briefcases, stiff upper lips, and large war toys, I knew something they didn't? It could. Could it be that the increasing threat of violence at every level from neighborhood to nation had something to do with the absence of women from the action? It could. This was a frightening idea for me; I wanted to keep on seeing the emperor's new clothes. But it was clear that the ancient male programming that worked for killing mastodons and shooting crossbows was no longer survival-efficient.

It now seemed so obvious: women (particularly mature women with time and experience) *had* to get "out there." But it seemed unlikely that we could even address this problem, much less make a real contribution, as long as we ourselves bought the idea that we were "over the hill."

The youth fixation is not a "woman's problem." It is more accurate to call it the symptom of a system of gender arrangements that is obsolete, injurious to both sexes, and dangerous to human survival. Our species can no longer afford to deprive half of its members of living fully while the other half attempts the impossible task of carrying the world, Atlas-like, on its shoulders. In the words of Dorothy Dinnerstein, we are all letting "the fate of our species slip through our fingers: the males, through inadequate contact with survival-essential considerations; and the females, through inadequate authority to make public policy."

The writing of this book had taken on a new urgency for me. I wanted as many women as possible to see what they were doing to themselves every day of their lives that limited who they were and could be. I wanted to break the taboo against admitting our youth hangup, so that we could deal with it. I wanted us to stop feeling ashamed of the natural process of aging. And I wanted us to create a context for making the public contribution that is as much our responsibility as it is our right.

To write about women and aging is to write about fear and hope. Fear of abandonment, of uselessness, of sexual frustration, of economic deprivation. These fears are real. But so are the possibilities for the future. Older women are currently our most underutilized natural resource—a resource we can no longer continue to neglect.

It is time to light up the dark side of the moon.

1

ROUND PEGS
IN SQUARE HOLES

The Double Standard of Aging

Young and pretty women may delude themselves about the amount of abuse meted out to women, for as long as they are young and pretty, they escape most of it.

—Germaine Greer

There is good reason to be apprehensive about aging if you are female—not because of wrinkles and gray hairs, but because of the fall from grace they represent.

My wealthy, divorced friend Lee found this out one evening when she was swept away in a moment of passion with a man about her age: forty-five. The moment had arrived to move from a nude clinch on the floor to the bed—which happened to be a loft accessible by a ladder. Lee went first. When they reached the top, her lover's face wore a strange expression. To her inquiry, he reluctantly replied, "I saw something that turned me off." Lee realized that what he had seen was her no-longer-twenty-five-year-old rear end mounting the ladder. "I learned from that never to go first," she laughed. But her humor did not conceal her hurt.

Lee had learned never to go first because she was no longer first. That place now belonged to younger women. We hesitate to talk about this openly, but even those of us who are presently secure and successful know we risk being bumped off the ladder. A well-known woman author in her forties who I thought had everything surprised me when she suddenly said, "How I hate them—these young women walking along the street as if they owned it! They have something I'll never have." The thing they had, of course, was youth. At that moment, it did not occur to her that she also had something they didn't: age.

Age is perceived not as an asset but as a liability for women. Men are thought to gain the poise of maturity, while women lose the freshness of youth. This double standard of aging, as Susan Sontag called it, is a fact of life for women as well as men. "Aging doesn't bother me," one man told me. "But writing about women and aging—now there's a depressing subject." We may decry this double standard, dismiss it, or even endorse it, but at the very least we all acknowledge its existence.

It touches some women subtly, lightly—and literally kills others of us. Few escape scot-free. It touched Marjorie at sixty-one, the brilliant wife of a university professor whose career she had fostered—when she was found dead from an overdose of drugs. It touched Alice, fifty-one, when she found she could not stop crying after a "routine" hysterectomy. Touched Jane, thirty-five, a designer, when she felt invisible at an office cocktail party and drank too much. Touched Althea, sixty-five, when she found herself thrown out on the street, homeless, because she was unable to pay her rent.

The double standard of aging is a prejudicial attitude—and also a harsh economic reality. In a land which neglects its elders, women bear the brunt of this mistreatment. If men married women older than themselves, or if women could remarry as easily as men do and earn what they earn, the situation would be different today. As it is, the dependent status of women and the double standard of aging make us the fastest-growing poverty group in the nation. Statistics from the Census Bureau and Department of Labor are ultimate sources: 72 percent of American elderly poor, that is, people over 65, are women.

It is projected that one out of four working women will be poor in old age (over 65).

Now that the minimum $122 Social Security benefit has been

eliminated, 89 percent of those affected have been shown to be older women.

One often hears that "the wealth of America is in the hands of older women." If so, that is news to those of us who make up the largest and poorest minority in America. Wealth is certainly not in the hands of those homeless women who are now taking their place on America's breadlines, along with the underclass of males who traditionally have used these services. These women have become so numerous and visible that they even have earned a nickname: "shopping bag ladies."

But even if we are not at the bottom, we are still likely to feel the economic effects of the double standard. We fall through the cracks in our economic system in any number of ways. First, work in the home is not officially considered work at all. The Social Security system, for example, recognizes only outside employment as work. One woman, Diana Smith Yackel, writing in *Prime Time*, tells how she called the Social Security office after her mother's death to see if there was a death benefit accruing to her. As she waited on the phone, she reminisced about her mother's life:

> My town-bred mother learned to set hens and raise chickens, feed pigs, milk cows, plant and harvest a garden, and can every fruit and vegetable she could scrounge. She carried water a quarter of a mile from the well to fill her wash boilers ... she chopped out 40 acres of Canadian thistles with a hoe.... From her wheelchair she canned pickles, baked bread, ironed clothes, wrote dozens of letters to her friends and half a dozen or more kids.... "I think I've found your mother's records," said the [Social Security] employee. "Your mother isn't entitled to our death benefit." "Not entitled! But why?" The voice on the telephone is very assured and explains patiently, "Well, you see, your mother never worked."

Second, the female pattern of interrupted employment is a huge handicap in our male-geared system. The stubborn fact that women earn only 59 percent of what men earn is partly due to women's absence from the labor force during the crucial decade (twenty-five to thirty-five years of age) when advancement is most rapid. Not too many older women, except the poorest paid, were in the job market during those years. This broken employment pattern also reduces retirement benefits, which are geared to continuous work histories.

Third is the impact of the double standard on our couple-oriented system. In today's freewheeling climate, many women realistically fear they will lose their job as wife to a younger woman. New "no fault" divorce laws are being used by men to unilaterally unload their older wives. These women find that twenty-five years of faithful service carries with it little or no security. The fear of aging, then, often has an economic base even among women who are financially secure.

The dependency of the married state is a mixed blessing. Married women over forty are well aware that their future depends upon the health, financial fortunes, and good graces of their husbands. We will never know how many stay in destructive or dead-end marriages out of fear that they will not be able to survive economically on their own. Or even the effect on a good marriage when a wife has to think of her husband not only as a partner but also as a meal ticket.

Her fears are justified. The Older Women's League estimates that there are 4 million "displaced homemakers" who are thrown on the job market with little or no preparation. Many of these widows and divorcees are shocked to find that they are no longer covered by their husbands' pension plans, health insurance, or Social Security.

And when they look for work, they find that many jobs are open only to women who are considered "decorative." Although against the law, age discrimination cannot be legislated away. In Studs Terkel's *Working*, an advertising executive says:

In a profession where I absolutely cannot age, I cannot be doing this at 38. Although I'm holding this job on talent and responsibility, I got here partly because I'm attractive and it's a big kick for a client to know that for three days in Montreal there's going to be this young brunette, who's very good, mind you. I don't know how they talk about me, but I'd guess: she's very good, but to look at her you'd never know it. She's a knockout.

And Laurie Shields writes in her book, *Displaced Homemakers*:

Whatever doubts raised by my unsuccessful attempts to resume the career in advertising I'd abandoned when married, the idea of being "too old" wasn't one of them. The manager of a small San Francisco agency broke it to me tactfully, and all things considered, gently. . . . Dropping her eyes to the material on the desk, she continued, "Perhaps I shouldn't say this, but I'm 48" (long pause); "and unfortunately, in this city . . . that's pretty much over the hill for most jobs. Not that anyone would come out and say so because it's against the law . . ."

And an Englishwoman reports:

I inquired if a certain firm in which I was interested had a suitable post a short while ago; I gave them a full rundown of what I could do and had done, and I look good on paper. They were very enthusiastic and said that they had such a post coming up shortly and were most interested; would I just fill in the enclosed form. I sent it off post-haste. Two weeks later, without even an interview, I was told that they had filled the post. The only difference between my original letter and the form was a space for my age!

Humbler jobs are also affected. The "cute" young waitress is given the "good" tables; the older woman is relegated to the night shift. "People like to see a pretty face," she is told.

When these economic effects are taken together, we see that the "plight of the aged" is a women's problem to a degree not usually recognized. For women between the ages of forty-five and sixty-four, the mean income is $8,900 (for men in this age range it is almost twice as much). This group includes many single women, since only 32 percent of women over forty remarry. And after sixty-five, the situation deteriorates rapidly. One out of every four women still at work can look forward to living in poverty after sixty-five. The median income for all these females is $3,087, and for black women, $2,385.

Singledom marks an abrupt fall from grace for many women who were not formerly poor. The average age of widowhood is fifty-six, and three-fifths of all women over sixty-five are unmarried, while three-fourths of men over sixty-five live with their spouses. The social and sexual plight of single older women is compounded by their economic situation. One-third of all widows are below the poverty line and their ranks are growing.

Statistics are authoritative, but they do not convey human suffering. A short time ago, a bent old woman whose name I never learned asked me to help her across the street. "I can no longer depend on my eyes," she said. As we waited for her bus, she told me how her husband had died some years ago, how she had no children—nobody, in fact. How she lived in a rented room she could no longer afford. "It's hard when you get old," she added. "Is it worth it?" I asked bluntly. She paused and her faded eyes suddenly gleamed at me. "No, I don't think so," she said quietly. "I'd just as soon be on my way. Yes, I'd just as soon be on my way," she repeated. "But what can I do?" We sat in silence and as I groped for words, the bus came and she was gone.

Aside from its economic effects, the double standard of aging breeds hopelessness, uselessness, and sexual and social isolation for untold numbers of women. Given these pressures, it is not surprising that prime time for "nervous breakdowns" and suicide for women is from the late forties to the mid-sixties.

Our production-oriented societies dehumanize the old of both sexes, but women are helped onto the shelf while still in their prime. A Parisian woman who heard I was writing about women over forty said, "Oh, you are writing about retirement." "Retirement?" "Mais oui, forty is the retirement age for women."

It is true that men—especially working men—are also heavily penalized for aging, and that some women today "beat the system." Nevertheless, the system is alive and well. In general, women lose their sexual, economic, and social clout at a time when men are most fully coming into their own. This fact is publicly denied, ignored, and misunderstood to an amazing degree.

When I told a prominent woman photographer of forty about the thesis of my book, her reply was, "But all my friends are in their forties and one is a famous writer, one an editor, one a painter, etc." This denial that a problem exists is common among the vanguard who have achieved success; they see only the positive changes.

These changes are real and exciting. This book, for example, would not have been published ten years ago. And we need to be aware of our new options—without echoing male denials that there is a problem. For even the most secure among us know that somewhere we are vulnerable as long as the double standard of aging exists—if only in our fears of what the future may bring.

New Possibilities

But as we confront the despair that our situation engenders, we also recognize a source of hope. This hope springs from the fact that, though we are neglected by a society that adulates the young and the male, we are also the largest and fastest-growing segment of that society.

Growing numbers leads to growing awareness. We know that we are not alone in our sufferings. Our personal feelings are not due to personal failure. We did not invent the double standard of aging, and we don't have to add to our troubles by blaming ourselves for them. We can, however, shape our futures if we understand our situation and deal with it as a collective opportunity.

Never before have so many of us been able to anticipate a long and liberated life—whose culmination will probably be spent alone. Never before have so many of us had so many years to look forward to—and so little cultural direction about how to live them meaningfully. Society gives us few answers to the question: What shall I do with the rest of my life?

In fact, our growing numbers baffle a culture that does not know what to do with us. It is almost as if our social institutions have not caught up with the fact that older women are a growing force that is here to stay. Society still treats us like guests who have tactlessly worn out our welcome. We are seen not as a resource, but as a "problem." The only answers to our question about the purpose of our lives will have to come from ourselves. This is baffling—but also exciting.

More than 35 million American women are now forty-five years old or older. This makes us 32 percent of the female population; in 1900 we were only 9 percent. The longevity curve has been inching steadily upward, and by the year 2000 one in eight Americans will be sixty-five or over. But for women the curve is not inching but leaping. Generally, women live now almost ten years longer than men—on the average until age seventy-one. By age sixty-five there are two women to every man.

We take women's longevity for granted, but it is a relatively new phenomenon. Before the turn of the century, life expectancy was no higher for women than for men (which still remains the case in a few countries like Upper Volta and India). Women were hardest hit during the childbearing years—the most dangerous part of a woman's life. By age thirty the mortality rate for women was 12 percent higher than for men, largely as a result of complications of pregnancy. The widower used to be a prominent stock character in history, literature, and legend. Fairy tales are full of Cinderellas who lost their natural mothers in childbed; turn-of-the-century diaries and chronicles tell of widowers who have remarried—often several times—after the death of their young brides. Happily, birth control, modern medical care, and healthier life styles have made such stories anachronisms.

Not only do we have more years to live, but we are spending fewer of them being mothers. This is due in part to the dramatic drop in infant mortality. Our grandmothers' lives were shaped by the fact that they could not reasonably hope to raise more than half the children they bore. They spent their lives being pregnant, bearing and losing children, tied to the birth cycle and resigned to lives contingent upon the fates. Today the future of our children is still threatened by potential catastrophes, but infant mortality is not one of them unless we are poor. Our children are likely to survive their childhood, and so are we; our grandmothers arrived at midlife exhausted from their labors and already old.

Most of us are having fewer children, thanks to birth control. And some of us are forgoing motherhood altogether. Since our reproductive lives are occupying a shorter part of our life span, most women over forty can look forward to living almost as long again in good health, and without major child-care responsibilities.

This combination of growing numbers, improved health and fitness, longer life, and reproductive freedom is unprecedented for our species. And if we add our high divorce rate and geographic mobility to this picture, a critical mass of older women emerges that live differently from older women of previous generations.

For one thing, we work. The sixties saw an enormous influx of women into the labor force, with older women in the lead. From 1890 to 1960, the proportion of working women aged forty-five to fifty-four jumped from 11 percent to 52 percent. True, the jobs we get are often the humblest. In fact, all the lowest-paid occupations, apart from farm labor, are "women's work": practical nurses, hairdressers, health aides, nurses' aides, sewing workers, school monitors, child-care workers. But our participation in the labor force at all represents a huge change in the patterning of our lives.

In our society a paycheck represents adulthood and personal worth, and a woman who works thinks differently about herself. As one woman said: "I could not get any work at first besides a shit job filing that paid the minimum wage. Perhaps I didn't really think I deserved more. But once I started, I compared myself to people around me who were earning double my salary. After four months, I decided to quit. I knew I could do better and was ready to go pound on some doors and sell myself."

Not only do we live differently; we expect more from life. Pat Durham, an energetic woman in her mid-forties, exemplifies this new breed. She has learned to keep her arthritis under control with daily exercise. Pat spent many years raising kids, teaching physical education, and conducting a mail order business. Now separated from her husband, she is living in a communal household with other adults, and is a coordinator of Options for Women Over Forty, an organization dedicated to assisting older women to find work, housing, and community. "I feel a new openness toward life that I want to keep," says Pat. "I really wonder what other untouched parts of me there are that it will take a new experience to open."

Like Pat Durham, women are as a group better educated, healthier, and more articulate than ever before. When Gloria Steinem replied "This *is* forty-two" to the usual so-called compliment that she did not look her age, she was speaking from the new sense of vitality that many older women feel—and project. Most of us can sense the gap between ourselves and our mother's generation.

The rate of change is dizzying. I remember a radio "soap" I used to listen to as a child called *The Romance of Helen Trent*, "the story of a woman who will not let life pass her by." The announcer went on to reassure us that "although life mocks her, breaks her hopes, dashes her against the rocks of despair, she fights back bravely, *successfully*, to prove what so many women want to prove in their own lives: *that romance can live in life at thirty-five and beyond.*"

Helen was a harbinger of today's "midlife woman." But she felt intimations of midlife at thirty-five. By today's standards, she would be considered in her prime, a full-fledged member of the Pepsi generation. "Midlife" is shifting upward so rapidly that during the period of the writing of this book I sensed it moving from forty closer to fifty. The authors of *Hitting Our Stride*, a midlife study, see the same trend; Joan Cohen, Karen Levin, and Joan Pearlman state that nearly three-quarters of their interviewees (who tended to be young, fortyish, and well educated) felt themselves to be "younger" than their chronological age. This discrepancy suggests rapid social change.

We are moving very fast—both because we seek new roles and because the old ones are becoming obsolete. We are perhaps the fastest-changing segment of a society itself in the throes of constant change. This can be a very uncomfortable feeling—what Alvin Toffler describes as "future shock," i.e., the malady caused by change too rapid to assimilate.

Some women resolve this confusion by retreating into a new conservatism, digging in their heels and understandably decrying the lack of security that women face today. Often these are women with less opportunity to profit from the new options. But though they feel that the answer lies in a return to traditional values, their methods have a distinctly feminist flavor. For all their protestations, even the Phyllis Schlaflys and Marabel Morgans among us are not themselves in the kitchen, quietly complaining to their neighbors. Their assertive *style* may ultimately have more impact than the values they endorse.

Others of us are aware that there is no going back. For the first time, we see ourselves as cultural innovators, rather than as pegs that fit holes already drilled. But in our search to capitalize on our alternatives, we often are confused about our situation. The two messages of despair and hope are difficult to sort out.

Double Messages

We are caught between these messages, one positive, one negative.

Are we enjoying our "golden years," as many books attest? Or are we society's neglected, lonely leftovers? Are we finding that "sex is better than ever," as newspaper features report? Or are we eating dog food in rooming houses? Are we riding motorcycles and having lovers of thirty? Or are we displaced homemakers, thrown on the job market with no skills? Are we taking advantage of the exciting new opportunities opening up for older women in many fields? Or are we beating a retreat, fearful of independence?

These conflicting messages confuse us, depress us, make us hopeful, make us frightened, convince us that it is not our fault, that it is all our fault. We don't know whether to be angry at the discrimination we endure or to blame ourselves because we don't look like Jane Fonda or make $50,000 a year.

To arrive at an overview, we will first need to understand the sources of the double standard of aging in our society.

Agism and Sexism, American Style

The double standard of aging is compounded of equal parts agism and sexism. Despite its manifold advantages, America provides a perfect medium for the growth of these two virulent bacteria. Taken individually they are devastating enough. Taken together—and in women they are always taken together—their combined toxicity permeates our atmosphere so thoroughly that we may not even notice it. But as older women we absorb it with each breath.

Age discrimination, as we have seen, weighs more heavily on women than on men. And sexism is inherently agist, because the tits-and-ass mentality equates female value with female youthfulness.

This association of female attractiveness with youthfulness, in fact with childishness, manifests in many areas of our culture. Women are called "baby"; the ideal of beauty is often a childlike look—wide eyes, rosy cheeks, tiny nose, cute little pout. Styles considered fetching on adult women are often designed to mimic little girls—flat chests, ruffles and bows, pony tails, short skirts. One study found that the white female teenage face was rated most attractive by judges of all ages, races, and sexes. But you don't have to read research to know how inordinately our culture values child-women. Just look at Brooke Shields.

If women can be made to seem like children they can be more easily controlled, and this inferior position can be made to seem more acceptable. Thus female attractiveness, and femaleness itself, becomes associated with youth for reasons of dominance as well as reproduction. Woman comes to "mean," in essence, young woman.

This climate creates an information blackout on the conditions of older women. Statistics on women in general often overlook the special situation of older women. Even many so-called feminist analyses neglect to mention age discrimination against women or to index this separately. And statistical studies of older Americans make a false assumption of homogeneity, failing to differentiate between men and women, although their situations are not the same. Statistical invisibility of course means invisibility in the minds of legislators and social planners. The very choice of age sixty-five for "senior citizen" status is a male-determined choice, since the age-related problems of women start much earlier than this.

Agism is, in fact, the last bastion of sexism. As all women grudgingly are granted the right, if not the reality, of economic opportunity, the last mental barrier to equality is the almost visceral disgust for the older woman as a physical being. It is almost as if society says, yes, I'm all for giving them equal rights—but would you want your son to have an affair with one?

Bearing in mind the linkage between these two forms of bias, we will look first at agism and then at sexism to clarify their impact upon us.

Agism

The word "agism" was coined by the psychiatrist Robert Butler to describe the attitude that older people are inferior. Our institutions are shaped by this attitude; we think "young" just as we think "white" and "male."

Agism is not only an attitude of the young—in fact there is probably no other form of discrimination so meekly accepted by its victims. Surveys such as the Harris poll indicate that the negative attitudes toward old people held by the public are also widely endorsed by old people, although they personally consider themselves exceptions. They agree with the public that as a group they are "unalert," "closed-minded," and "less good at getting things done." They feel even more strongly than the general population that they are "less warm and friendly."

And older people reveal their agism in the way they acquiesce to their own ill-treatment. "Agism infects us," says Maggie Kuhn of the Gray Panthers, "when we despise our powerlessness, wrinkled skin and physical limitations. A symptom of our sickness is that we feel complimented when others tell us we do not look or act our age."

People feel differently in more age-positive cultures. For example, Native-American and Chinese women look forward to the time of life when they will become people of importance. In Sri Lanka, elders are addressed by the honorific "intelligent one." And in Northern Europe, most elders take for granted a level of economic security and personal respect much higher than our own.

Agism goes hand in hand with our economic system. Young people eat more, spend more, want more. They also produce more. The whole culture becomes geared to meeting their needs, and when these show signs of being met, to creating new ones. Their purchasing power makes them the favored darlings of the culture—and being the favored darlings of the culture, they also have more purchasing power. However, the demographic shift toward an older population, particularly now that the "baby boom" generation is approaching middle age, is giving older people more economic clout. This new power probably underlies the credibility of the older people's movement in recent years.

But in some respects, this economic explanation of agism is too simple. Why should older people be seen as such minimal consumers in the first place? Does our wisdom make us genuinely less materialistic? Or does the cultural admonition that older people *should* live economically restricted lives become a self-fulfilling hypothesis? After all, older people with money manage to spend and enjoy it like everyone else. It will take more than economic analysis to explain agism.

Agism is also the social face of the denial of mortality—that is, the cumulative outcome of not wanting to think about aging and dying. This universal human tendency, which will be discussed at length in the next chapter, is particularly at home in American culture. "Never say die" is our slogan. We think there are solutions to everything, even dying—and jump to facile concepts of "positive thinking" or an afterlife to avoid actually confronting the awe and terror that death inspires.

This sanguine outlook comes partly from our youth as a people. Older nations which have suffered the horrors of war, tyranny, and famine find our national optimism inconceivable. And our pioneer past leads us to believe that a brighter future is just around the corner—in fact, to feel differently seems vaguely unpatriotic. This ethos of youthful optimism is not supportive of facing personal aging—or of dealing with our elders.

The denial of mortality even colors our attempts to ameliorate the aging process. When youth-oriented scientists confront the problem of longevity, panic and denial rather than acceptance of aging dictate their response. This leads to a new gerontological technology that emphasizes quantity of years lived rather than quality of life. We already know that improvement in the quality of life directly increases longevity. Eating more wholesomely, exercising regularly, dealing with stress, and living purposefully are our best hope against the chronic degenerative disease killers of later life: heart disease, cancer, diabetes. But little energy is going into the development of innovative ways to implement this knowledge.

Instead, this new gerontology rejoices in its latest "breakthroughs." We are told we can look forward to gene splicing to adapt us to environmental conditions now untenable for human life, electrodes implanted inside the skull to alter the biological clock, and organ cloning to replace any diseased organ a theoretically infinite number of times. What psychiatrist Robert Butler, an expert on aging, calls the "basic fairness" of ceding the planet to the next generation is becoming eroded. And questions about purpose and meaning in this long life are not being addressed.

Change, youth, and novelty are ironically traditional values here, revered right along with Thanksgiving. As a nation of immigrants, the young are looked to as the standard-bearers of the culture. My mother's generation wanted to be "up to date," so they could "shimmy like my sister Kate." We all still want to be "with it," whatever "it" is. It is perhaps inevitable that such values lead to agism, since the contributions of the old are perceived as obsolete.

Because of our heritage of rugged individualism, we also value self-reliance inordinately and question any kind of dependency.

Even the natural dependency of advancing age seems somehow shameful. We recoil from reminders of bodily function and imperfection; the fat, the ugly, the deformed, the handicapped—and the old—are cosmeticized or banished from view. A decorous lengthening of garments covers the years; even minor signs of aging are somehow embarrassing, like going outside with your slip showing. Feeling *shame* for aging is especially hard to admit, since it seems so irrational. Yet older people cover their stigmata on beaches and in parks, out of consideration for our squeamishness—and perhaps their own. Given this milieu, it shocked me pleasantly to visit an Indian pueblo and see aged people participating in the ceremonies, with a palsied man playing a leading role. In a land where even a misshapen apple or an uncapped tooth is becoming a rarity, we create a scatology of aging: exposing a flabby arm is like leaving the bathroom door open.

This national penchant for the pretty makes us hypocrites. We turn the old into what Simone de Beauvoir calls the Other not by insult but by flattery. In other words, we deny our denial. Not only do we want to shove aging into the closet, we also want to pretend that the closet isn't there. "Age means nothing," we say. "You are only as old as you feel." A plastic surgeon I interviewed said, "I never speak about middle age, only about middle youth." And if older people's problems actually intrude upon us, we blame *them*. "Aging is all a question of attitude," we say, as if the old could become young by a quick dose of positive thinking.

All these tendencies in our culture conspire to push old age under the rug. Like sex in Victorian times, we pretend it is simply "not done." Older people themselves report that they become invisible to others. A white-bearded friend described waiting in line at a supermarket checkout, when a young man cut in ahead of him with a pack of cigarettes, totally ignoring his existence. "Look, I'm too big to be invisible," he said. The young man looked as if he had been awakened from a dream and apologized profusely.

Our new living arrangements foster this invisibility. The multigenerational family unit is obsolete. Americans today move away from their parents, often ending up in age-segregated communities. Many young people barely know their grandparents, and studies reveal that negative stereotypes about age are widely held by college students. Actual contact with elderly persons shifted these beliefs in a positive direction, but in real life this kind of contact is rare. Our elders become isolated—either with their peers, or totally alone. Many of us know more people from other countries than we do older people. Thus, to find out how they are faring, we have to read books and studies, like anthropologists investigating exotic peoples. We cannot simply look around us.

Our agism is also clear in the design of our physical surroundings. The environment perceived through the eyes of an older person looks like a dangerous obstacle course. Older people are easy targets for crime on poorly policed and dimly lighted streets. They are yelled at by impatient bus drivers. Traffic lights turn red before they can get across the street. Stairs and slippery pavements are everywhere, while elevators, escalators, and ramps are often nonexistent in subways and other public places. It is no wonder that the elderly tend to remain in familiar, already-tested environments. They get the message: only the young are entitled to full participation in our society.

As we deny our elders, we get out of touch with what researcher Ken Dychtwald calls "the elder within," the part of ourselves that carries our expectations for the second half of our lives:

Just as we all have a "child within" whose character has been formed by the images and experiences of our youth, so we each have an "elder within," composed and constructed from the myths and beliefs we have about growing older. Many people never acknowledge or nourish this part of themselves, and so, not surprisingly, they wind up feeling enormously unprepared, angry, or depressed when they realize that they too are aging. But it's hard to admit to the feelings of loss, despair or helplessness that aging engenders when we know they may be seen as weakness, self-indulgence or "negativity." In our culture, denial masquerades as pluck, consideration of the young, and a "positive outlook."

Sexism

If we drew a "personal profile" of an ideal pioneer, he would have maximum freedom of movement, and be physically strong and adventurous. He would be individualistic, oriented to what works in the short run, and optimistic about the future. This personal profile does indeed suggest a "he"—a male body. The relative stability of this body over time and its exemption from cyclic change and childbearing would be distinct advantages in a situation where independence and physical prowess were needed. This body belongs to the American culture hero. It looms at us from billboards, magazines, movie and TV screens—wearing Western clothes, foreign-intrigue trenchcoats, army fatigues, and surgical scrub suits.

It is here between the lines of this Marine Corps advertisement:

> A Marine officer is a leader. He can manage. Himself, his men. His missions. A Marine officer is sure of himself. He welcomes challenge. He never takes the easy way out. A Marine officer is his own man. An individual. A Marine officer is imaginative. Resourceful. The spirit of "can-do" and "make-do" is as old as the Corps itself. A Marine officer is ambitious. To him status quo means nothing. He sets his sights on advancement. . . .

What is life like in the female body? It certainly differs from this male norm. These differences are usually equated with the childbearing function, but that is an agist perspective. It limits the "interesting difference" between women and men to the childbearing years, when a woman's bodily reality is significantly different from a man's every day of her life.

Change is the most constant reality of life in the female body. In addition to the monthly cycle, women's lives are characterized by successive physiological phases which divide their life span:

puberty, sexual initiation, maternity, menopause. These phases are experienced subjectively and also mark her body. The autopsy of an anonymous female would tell us, in addition to her age, her degree of sexual maturity, whether or not she was a virgin, whether she had had children and approximately how many, whether she had nursed them, whether she had reached menopause.

The interconnectedness of all life is also imprinted upon us. Men experience their bodies as discrete, unencumbered, bounded by their skin. But where does a woman's body stop and that of her child begin? She shares her womb with the child, the milk in her breasts, her very life. We never lose our knowledge that all life is one no matter how long we live.

Patriarchal cultures exaggerate the differences between the male and female body through education and socialization. But certain irreducible differences exist: women bear children and tend to have a smaller muscle mass than do men. All societies must take these differences into account; our society interprets them as liabilities. This interpretation can make us overlook the special advantages that life in the female body brings. These advantages only deepen with age.

The "personal profile" we could deduce from a female body would differ in some important respects from that of the young male. The person living in this body would be aware of her vulnerability and mutability. Respect for the cycles of nature and for the preciousness of life would be part of her bodily experience. She might tend to be more willing to acknowledge her limitations and to act interdependently, rather than alone. Her need for a social support system would lead her to develop sensitivity to others.

In addition, a woman's bodily adaptation to discontinuity teaches her flexibility as a style of life and work. In addition to the changes the childbearing cycle demands, she moves in and out of the labor force, often shifting roles with seeming ease. Although there is change on the horizon, she can do this because she usually doesn't identify with any particular role as much as with the "umbrella" role of being the facilitator; the mortar that holds the bricks together, the greaser of wheels. Women capitalize on their bodily adaptability when they get a chance to play roles that are not male-defined. Homemaking is one of them.

The usual list of a homemaker's jobs misses the point, because her real work is to be the weaver of the web that holds all the specifics together. She is the kinkeeper, the one who sustains the family and social network. Today she may take a job as a computer programmer to supplement the family's income. Fifty years ago, when the children were small, she may have taken in a boarder. One hundred years ago she may have raised a pig. It doesn't really matter. Shoelaces are replaced before they break, an errand is run for an old neighbor, the shelves are dusted. The school problem that might have developed doesn't because she was there to forestall it with her presence, and the cottage cheese that was going to spoil becomes a quiche instead. Her brain is like a computerized recycling center, registering scarcities and abundances, taking up the slack here, automatically adjusting the balance there, funneling the resources where they will do the most good. One scientist called her a "tension manager."

In the past, the more obvious household tasks women performed may have eclipsed her central facilitating function. Women used to have more tangible reasons to feel proud of their homemaking artistry, perhaps symbolized by the patchwork quilt—at once a superb example of recycling and a useful object which today commands high prices in art galleries. It is harder to feel the same pride after returning from a harrowing afternoon at the Sears white sale, taking a load of clothes from the dryer, watching the kids, noticing that a chair leg needs gluing, and telephoning Aunt Mary while thinking about dinner—yet the essence remains the same. Unfortunately, the world does not reward this kind of work. And the irony is, the better homemaking is performed, the less one sees it, like the glue holding together a beautifully mended vase.

It is also a natural and useful kind of work for older people, especially older women. Yet its invisibility contributes to their already low visibility. And today more than ever, it is becoming increasingly invisible as the parts of it that fit the standard "job description" are falling away. Women themselves may think of "real housework" as heavy-duty cooking, cleaning, washing—all of which are becoming less necessary, especially in the lives of older women. The vital facilitating function, however, is so automatic to women that they themselves may not even be aware that they are "doing anything." Work in our society is usually defined as effortful, divorced from daily life and measured by economic gain. By this definition a woman who spends her day facilitating may not feel she has been working.

The invisibility of women's work pervades even the business world. As one businesswoman said, "When men lunch together, they are having a conference; when women lunch together, they are gossiping."

Just as our environments are geared to youthfulness, they are also geared to maleness. Our society rigorously trains boys to suppress the "feminine" aspects of themselves. Being a "sissy" is never acceptable for boys, while being a "tomboy" is tolerated for girls. The result is a rejection of the values inherent in the female bodily experience, and a polarization of men and women into almost different species with different values, interests, and life styles—as the following letter illustrates.

Dear Abby:

Now that football training has nearly begun, I would like to bring up something that has bothered me for a long time. The boys love the sport and they love to win, but year after year they are told to "hit hard." As one coach told his team of 8-year-olds, "You'll know you've hit hard enough when you leave the other guy bleeding!" (This is building character?)

My son's coach tells the boys that they have to be mean to play good football. The "meanest" boys are praised, and the gentle ones are subjected to verbal degradation.

Many of the boys say they don't hit hard because they don't really want to hurt the other boy. Now maybe I've missed something somewhere along the line, but I think the child who doesn't want to hurt anybody seems to have the right idea.

One Lad's Mother

Men are expected to be always tough and hard, always in form, whether on the job, the playing field, or in bed. The male ideal of bodily continuity makes possible our bureaucracies and industrial plants, with their rigid schedules and imperviousness to human variability. Men suffer in these environments too, but for women they are especially inhospitable. Monthly cycles, pregnancy, nursing, and the vicissitudes of child care are treated as aberrations in this world. Opportunities to achieve a synthesis between work world and "woman's world" are rare. I did it inadvertently one day, with my friend Marilyn, who teaches graduate school. We were having a business lunch in downtown San Francisco, and as we walked back to our cars we passed a market that had excellent fruit. Without breaking stride we both calmly went inside fully aware of what our respective larders were lacking, made our purchases, and walked out while continuing our "professional" conversation.

The standard male perception of this incident would isolate certain aspects of Marilyn's and my interaction and call them "work" (the "professional" conversation and the actual shopping). This leaves out the crucial element of the initiative taken in noticing the fruit store, and the ability to capitalize on this opportunity, without detracting from our professional goal.

Our lunch combined the focused intellectuality easily attained in the male domain with the humanness of the female work style. But usually women are left out of the male world, or when included, are marginal to it. In that environment our bodies feel unreliable and inferior. We get little recognition for our gifts of mutability and interdependence. We are the round pegs that don't fit the square holes of a system geared to the young and the male.

The Enshrinement of Fertility

Agism and sexism create a milieu which is inhospitable to the older female bodily experience. If not for its reproductive function, the female experience would be totally invisible and unacknowledged by society. However, the period of reproductive activity, about one-third of a woman's total life span, is considered a sacrosanct domain.

At puberty, a woman comes into her own, socially speaking, and is noticed, protected, idolized, spoiled, and exploited too— insofar as she is gifted with the fertility-linked secondary sexual characteristics that we call beauty. So valuable is this period that twelve-year-olds try to get there before their time. Play makeup, the newest toy on the market, is selling well. And older women of course fight to stay this side of the hill. Schopenhauer's infamous dictum that "when children are no longer desirable, women are no longer necessary" still holds true. As our fertility and the hallmarks of it disappear, we become irrelevant and invisible.

This enshrinement of fertility is at the heart of the double standard of aging. A man's "prime" corresponds to his economic peak—at age forty or even later. But a woman's "prime" corresponds to her reproductive peak—in her twenties. Women get pushed into the category of nonpersons our society calls older people twenty years or so before men do.

The widely held myth that "men age better than women" is an expression of this double standard. Men do not age better than women—quite the reverse. A woman of forty or fifty is at least as physically competent as a man of the same age. Given women's longer life span, she is in fact probably biologically "younger" than her male peer. And her lifelong adaptation to bodily change leads her to take physical aging in her stride—as many women manage to do, in spite of the enormous handicap of the double standard of aging.

It is true that her childbearing days are over, since nature has wisely determined that the carriers of the species be at their physical peak. But a man of forty or fifty has also passed his physical and sexual peak in many respects. However, the myth persists, in spite of all evidence to the contrary. Imagine a man of forty with gray hair, a few wrinkles, and a bit of extra weight. Now imagine him becoming a woman with the same characteristics. Did he lose something with this sex change—a bit of youthfulness, attractiveness, interest, prestige? The myth is powerful, and permeates even our own perceptions.

The myth ties vitality to reproductive capacity—which, of course, the midlife male continues to experience. This bias was well illustrated by a male gynecologist. During a conversation about causes of menopause-related problems, he said, "Well, you must remember that most species end their lives shortly after reproductive capacity declines." This shocking statement implied that women's longevity was a sort of unnatural artifact and that disease after menopause was normal because we had fulfilled our function. I switched gynecologists.

But women cannot so easily escape the burden of this myth. How it affects us and how we respond to it will be explored at length in later chapters. But first, we will look at aging both as a human condition and as a male condition in order to understand why women get saddled so disproportionately with its onus.

2

BUT WE ALL GET OLDER: AGING AND THE HUMAN CONDITION

We must stop cheating: the whole meaning of our life is in question in the future that is waiting for us. If we do not know what we are going to be, we cannot know what we are: let us recognize ourselves in this old man or in that old woman.
Simone de Beauvoir in *Old Age*

Mortality vs. Aging

"I'm prepared to die," said my friend Hilda, "but not to look lousy for the next forty years." For all of us, aging and dying are related, but separate, realities. Mortality can be an abstraction, a change of state from being to nonbeing, while aging is concrete and personal—a process that happens to human bodies. Mortality inspires poetry and philosophy; aging calls forth visions of bridgework and varicose veins. Thinking about mortality implies actively dealing with the idea of one's nonexistence. Aging, on the other hand, evokes a process that we suffer passively.

Mortality has been portrayed as the cosmic question men must grapple with, while aging is seen as a mere women's woe. We think of Socrates and Xanthippe, that odd couple. He stands for everything that is noble about mortality, including a freely chosen death. Socrates transcends aging. And Xanthippe? She comes to us as an early image of the ball and chain, the shrew. Is she in menopause? Are her hemorrhoids bothering her? What does the old bag want, we wonder, if we stop to think about her at all, which is unlikely? Her sole fate is to be the old woman who constantly drags down the hero.

Even today, our conventional wisdom tells us that doctors (male) perform heroic procedures to cheat death, while nurses (female) tend the terminally ill. That men challenge their mortality on mountaintops and battlefields, while women take care of aging parents or cry over gray hairs. The implication is that the Big Abstraction of life vs. death belongs in the male province (as do all issues connected with our generic humanity); that women do not have the same need to ask the "big questions," either out of disinterest, stupidity, or being already "in harmony with nature." In any case, men have staked out the territory as their own.

However, women are also conscious beings, struggling with mortality, not daisies that bloom, wither, and die. We too know the anxiety articulated by Sally: "I was with my father-in-law when he died. The silence that fell then was different from the silence of living. That silence haunts me."

Yet for many of us, both male and female, aging may be more difficult to confront than mortality. The fear of a prolonged period of deterioration, dependency, or unattractiveness can seem worse than death itself. And the writer Florida Scott-Maxwell says:

> I don't like to write this down, yet it is much in the minds of the old. We wonder how much older we have to become, and what degree of decay we have to endure. We keep whispering to ourselves, "Is this age yet? How far must I go?" For age can be dreaded more than death. . . . It is waiting for death that wears us down, and the distaste for what we may become.

Until about twenty years ago, little effort was made to determine the causes of aging or death in human beings. Aging was taken for granted, although human aging is remarkable and unique. We are the only animals known to endure long past our reproductive years, outliving any other mammals of comparable size.

The causes of aging are still being debated. But it has been discovered that many of our common ideas about it have more to do with disease than with the increase of years. Most of us fall short of our potential 130 years due to chronic degenerative diseases that theoretically can be abolished. Would we then live in good health until the day we fell apart, like the Wonderful One Hoss Shay? Most of us have trouble even imagining what disease-free old age would be like.

The inaccurate stereotype that aging inevitably means falling apart is widespread. But aging as we know it is shaped by our culture, and can change as our culture changes. For example, until recently it was thought that muscle tissue "naturally" deteriorated after the mid-twenties, and that menopause meant weight gain. Current trends toward physical fitness and active life styles have shown these assumptions to be false. And aging can vary markedly from person to person. Older people actually become more diverse with advancing years, according to aging specialist Robert Butler. There are extraordinarily "young" eighty-year-olds as well as "old" eighty-year-olds. As the story goes, a woman went to the doctor with a painful right knee. "You're seventy years old, what do you expect?" he asked. "My left knee is also seventy, and it's fine," she replied.

The body is in constant change, and where we begin to call this change "aging" is somewhat arbitrary. Nevertheless, as the years pass, slowing down and wear and tear impinge increasingly upon our minds and bodies. Many of these changes are only minimally bothersome, particularly if our health is good. And for some of us, the advantages of a greater maturity outweigh the problems of aging. "I've *earned* being old—don't deprive me of that," says May Sarton.

But whether we are well or ill, at the gut (biological) level, aging means confronting our mortality, not as an abstraction, but with its full complement of messiness and vulnerability. The signs of age remind us all that we are not in control of what concerns us most: our life. And philosophers throughout history have discussed the central human irony that although we, like all animals, are programmed at our deepest levels for survival, it is only we, among all animals, who know that we will die.

The signs of aging rub our noses in this ironic situation. We feel the *unfairness* of it all: just as we finally are mastering this art called living, the body is betraying us by falling apart. Shortly before her death, the folk singer Malvina Reynolds put it this way: "Sometimes it seems like such a waste that all of a person's wisdom, skill and individuality should be wiped out just when it might do some good."

We are totally committed to a project—the development of the self—for which we know the ultimate grant will not be renewed. In view of this impending expiration date, our position of total identification with the project seems a bit ridiculous. It's no wonder that we view the signs of age with loathing; they remind us of our own absurdity.

From this bleaker viewpoint, each year lived is one year less to live. Over and above dealing with the loss of optimal physical functioning, then, is the loss of the illusion of immortality: the end of "happily ever after" and of the notion that I matter in any way proportional to my own self-involvement. I, who feel so much more important than this writing desk, that tree outside, or even the Taj Mahal, will be outlasted by them.

Mortality and Denial

For most people, the full experiencing of this loss is probably too overwhelming to endure, even when it is intellectually accepted. A few years ago, I was one of a group that cared for a wonderful woman who had chosen to end her life at home, surrounded by friends and family. Florence was dying of cancer and had elected to receive oxygen but no other supports. We took turns sitting with her, doing the necessary menial tasks and witnessing her gradual detachment from life. It was a long, tiring process; I rather congratulated myself on my ability to "face death and not fall apart."

One night, after a long day with Florence and her husband, I woke up and stumbled into the bathroom, my coping mechanisms in abeyance. I sat down in that most humbling of human positions and glanced out the window at the black sky. Suddenly I was shaking, weeping, my teeth chattering as I saw before me the dreadful truth: I was no less mortal than Florence was; I too would die.

Inadvertently I had faced the blackness—but not for long. Within minutes, the vividness of my feelings began to fade. I could feel my old denial mechanisms reactivating, and I told myself, "Remember how it felt to be aware of your death." And so I retell this incident as a memory—a memory of how it feels to be momentarily aware of one's transience, but especially a memory of how quickly that knowledge was denied and sealed over.

Denial is our first line of defense against the trauma of loss. Severe personal loss is literally a physical insult. All systems of the body are affected, notably the immune system, which may explain why there is such a high incidence of cancer among the bereaved.

Denial can take strange forms. Mother cats who have lost kittens perform endless "searching" rituals, going back again and again over the same territory as if to say, "I can't believe they're gone." A mother whose child has lost a leg and is dying of cancer talks about him as "handicapped."

We resist believing the worst, no matter how obvious it is, a fact which Hitler capitalized on. We see the same thing today when governments talk about civil defense precautions in case of atomic attack—a purely ritual gesture to reassure ourselves that a nuclear crisis would be no worse than other crises we have weathered in the past.

Denial works, according to psychiatrist Irving Yalom, because we have never quite outgrown our childhood belief in our omnipotence. Ever since our infant wails miraculously produced breakfast, a part of us still believes that wishing will make it so.

Like death itself, the aging process evokes denial. We make the older person into de Beauvoir's Other: the not-quite-human, the "dirty old man," the "little old lady in tennis shoes." When I was at college, the students called the middle-aged women who cleaned the dorms "biddies." And our euphemism "senior citizen" is equally impersonal and dehumanizing.

Simply to classify some people at an arbitrary age into another category paves the way for thinking of them as nonpersons. If we call ourselves "midlife women," for example, that can delude us into thinking of "older women" as a far-off category of sixty-five or more, thus alienating ourselves from our own future. For this reason, it may be less misleading to emphasize the life span as a continuity rather than as a series of stages. Aging, after all, is something we all have in common, yet we use it to divide us.

Denial dissociates us from the Other and also from our own bodies. We often experience the changes of aging as somehow alien to us, as if the "real self" is frozen in time, imprisoned somewhere within the aging body. A middle-aged woman I know said her older brother told her, "It's still me in here, you know," and then she added, "It's hard on them when they get older." *They.*

When we bury our dead we often bury our most recent memories of them. My aunt carries a wallet-size photo of her husband in middle age; he died at seventy-four. And in certain cemeteries, I have seen enameled photos embedded in the tombstones which make them monuments to denial. The portraits chosen rarely correspond to the date of death on the stones. Instead, an earlier, emblematic moment has been chosen: the vigorous father, the young mother. (The women especially are never old.) These cemeteries would seem to be filled with people cut down in their youth by some mysterious plague.

People become angry when their denial system is threatened. When de Beauvoir wrote that she felt old at fifty, she received volumes of criticism. Her readers did not want her to mourn her lost youth or admit the encroachments of time.

Denial and Middle Age

Eda LeShan, a journalist, remembers waking up one morning, "finding my elbows and fingers were very stiff and painful . . . I had a sense of physical aging and deterioration which terrified me. Part of me thinks of old age as a total disaster, and I am horrified by it."

To be young is to be immortal. Most of us who do begin to deal with mortality are spurred on by its intrusion at midlife. We then catch glimpses of the disgust and terror that are behind the denial.

Aging and dying are no longer ridiculous abstractions at middle age. The old woman whom I helped across the street could someday be me. I remember my grandmother, bent with arthritis; and now my mother resembles her. Will I too look this way before long? The thought intrudes with a relentless logic, puncturing my defenses.

Breaches in the wall of denial can be—and often are—sealed over. Yet the task of the second half of life is to come to terms with an increasingly limited life span, according to Butler. He goes on to say that the old in particular must learn *not* to think in terms of a future. Yet this can be difficult. A New Mexico widow told me:

> Dad was a great one for making plans. Next year we'll buy a mobile home, travel around the country. "Next year . . ." he was always saying. Well, when he got cancer he had this particular expression on his face toward the end. It's hard to describe . . . kind of like a kid looks when he tastes cotton candy. You know, a look that says "You mean, this is all there is to it?" He had that same expression on his face. I'll never forget it.

This man's dilemma and ours are the same, no matter what our age. Living always for the future diminished his present, so that when he reached the end, nothing was left. By living for the future, he was avoiding the present: denying his real age and pretending to himself that he had endless years ahead.

Denial of aging does not make us feel younger—quite the contrary. The awareness of our mortality gives each moment a precious intensity. This sense of truly living each moment is the essence of youthfulness.

As women, we also diminish our present by living in the past. For many of us, our real "golden years" were the years of fertility. If we fixate on them, we lose contact with both the fullness of the moment and the possibilities for the future. There is wisdom in the old saw "Where there's life there's hope."

Sometimes, a brush with death can shock us back to this innocent *joie de vivre* that is our birthright. It happened to me, shortly after I learned to drive, on an icy Boston highway. I was on my way to my job as a kindergarten teacher, when the car went into an uncontrolled skid. It spun round and round, and headed toward the side of the cliff. I heard myself scream and saw the picture of the wreck, like so many others, printed in the newspaper. "So this is how it happens," I thought, while screaming.

Suddenly it was all over. The car had hit a guard rail on the side of the cliff which had been invisible to me. I found myself sitting at right angles to the road with a destroyed automobile and a few minor bruises. A peculiar ordinariness immediately reasserted itself; the car behind me stopped and took me the rest of the way to school. There in my classroom the full awareness of my mortality broke through my denial and shock, and the miracle of life surged through me at the same moment. I irresistibly put on a record and when the children came in they found me dancing. "I'm dancing," I explained, "because I'm alive." No other explanation was necessary, as they joined in and danced with me.

The thoughts of death and aging are thrust out of consciousness. They become shadows, no longer subject to our control. There they grow, as shadows have a way of doing, and make common cause with all of our worst fantasy fears. As a man who sat with a dying friend told me:

Death was a thing I didn't particularly want to face; it seemed like this strange, weird thing to me. In my family it was like sex, the bathroom, and money—all hidden from me—so when I actually was at Lucy's deathbed I was surprised at how natural it seemed. It was an event, but almost the same kind of event as birth—not so special or cataclysmic, just part of the process. At one point she asked us to move back so that she could be alone, and her life force seemed to just gradually withdraw more and more into a dot until she was just a shell. There was no observable moment of transition.

The breakdown of denial at midlife gives us the opportunity to come to terms with our aging and dying—and thus to more fully experience our living. Our traditional mythologies are full of stories of people who take in the ugly or unacceptable, and in so doing, receive unexpected gifts. Beauty embraces the Beast; the Princess takes the frog to bed; our Old Testament forefathers welcomed the grime-covered travelers into their tents and found they were angels of the Lord. Only when this step is taken can the transformation take place.

Woman as Symbol of Aging

When Dostoyevsky's Raskolnikov wanted a victim for his premeditated, passionless crime, it was only natural that he choose an old woman: "a stupid, senseless old hag [who] does not even know what she is living for . . . she might just as easily die tomorrow."

The older woman is the symbol that falls most readily to hand for the worthless, expendable human being—the Other, the one who is not us. By focusing our fear and loathing of aging on her, we succeed in denying its reality for our own lives. And contemporary culture has perfected the means for efficient denial of aging: geriatric wards, golden-age ghettos, nursing homes. In the past the old were more difficult to put out of sight and out of mind, and perhaps people did not try as hard. To be genuinely old was a rarity and in some sense an achievement. The older person was in the mainstream of life, and therefore of literature and art as well.

Death was an ever-present hazard, due to the prevalence of infectious disease. The classics abound with references to aging and dying; life's brevity was a major literary theme. Gather ye rosebuds while ye may, we are told again and again.

The old were often caricatured, but they were at least in evidence. Female scolds and bawds, such as Chaucer's Wife of Bath, abound—but so do male dotards and cuckolds. The impotent older man and/or cuckold was in fact a standard figure of fun:

I slept with an old man all last night,
I turned to him and he turned to me,
He could not do so well as he might,
He tried and tried but it would not be.
[Madrigal]

Nevertheless, there is a sex-linked imbalance in traditional portrayals of the old. We find many positive portraits of older men—but virtually none of older women. And the most negative age-linked archetype of all is always female: the witch.

In preindustrial culture, male authors showed little interest in depicting older women except as caricatures. We look in vain for the female counterpart of Tiresias, Oedipus, Lear—characters that are admirable and at the same time human. The only exception I can think of are some of the female saints, whose lives are out of the mainstream. The absence of our literary grandmothers is painful.

When older women do make an appearance, they are usually ridiculed, like Xanthippe. The counterpart to the sage is the shrew.

The visual arts convey the same message. There are few positive images of older women. Church mosaics, for example, depict many sages—resplendent old men, wearing their years proudly. They symbolize transcendence of the body. But except for Mary, women hardly appear. And when they do they are either young or so lacking in individuation that it is hard to attach any age to them at all.

This tradition is so pervasive that we accept the ridiculously young Mary in Michelangelo's famous *Pietà*; the woman holding the dying Christ is far too young to be his mother. Evidently, the artist felt that Mary's transcendence could not be embodied in an older woman's image.

Older women are also often depicted as asexual, while older men never are. Pantaloon, the commedia dell'arte dirty old man (often shown with a huge dildo), clearly wants it—even if he can't get it up. Xanthippe and cohorts, however, are often neutered. Neither desirable nor desirous, they exist as pesky shadows on the dark side of the moon.

A neutered being is dehumanized, worthless. The most oppressive of social institutions (like concentration camps and old-style loony bins and prisons) have instinctively deprived women of the marks of femininity that foster respect and self-respect.

The only truly powerful symbol of older womankind we inherit is the witch:

The old woman, although her behavior was so kind, was a wicked witch, who lay in wait for children and had built the little house on purpose to entice them. When they were once inside she used to kill them, cook them, and eat them, and then it was a feast day with her.

The witch's eyes were red, and she could not see very far, but she had a keen scent, like the beasts, and knew very well when human creatures were so near.

["Hansel and Gretel"]

Sometimes she is wise and benevolent, but generally not. "Old," "ugly," and "evil" are synonyms in the Western folk tradition.

crone (O.Fr. *carogne*, carrion, carcass): thus a withered old woman.

hag: 1. originally a female demon or evil spirit. 2. a witch, enchantress. 3. an ugly repulsive old woman, especially an evil or malevolent one.

hagfish: n. any number of small eellike saltwater fishes (cyclostomes) with a round sucking mouth and horny teeth with which they bore into other fish and devour them.

[*Webster's New International Dictionary*]

We are the descendants of the witch-burners who killed two million women, primarily women living alone, i.e., spinsters and widows. According to Frazer, these folk also made wicker effigies ("wicca" is the old word for witch), containing live cats, which were burned—cats being the well-known companions of witches.

Witches are vengeful, envious of younger women, and baby-snatchers as well. Sleeping Beauty is cursed by one so that she will prick her finger with a spindle on her fifteenth birthday and fall down dead. "You may have as much rampion as you like," says the witch in "Rapunzel," "on one condition. The child that is born into the world must be given to me." The empty-nest syndrome epitomized.

Witchy-bitchy goddesses are also found in the Greco-Roman myths. Hera is the typical cast-off older wife who watches Zeus like a hawk and destroys whole populations out of jealous pique. (Jean Harris gained instant admission to the ranks of this archetype when she shot and killed her lover, "Diet Doctor" Herman Tarnower, for stepping out on her with a younger woman.)

To see women as witches is to see them as the Other—to deny their humanity. They then can be made into scapegoats for aging, for evil, and for destruction in our unconscious processes. The fear of aging gets dumped into the unconscious stew, where it simmers along with other repressed fears of women. Philip Wylie's *Generation of Vipers* exemplifies this process:

I give you mom. I give you the destroying mother. I give you death—the hundred million deaths that are muttered under Yggdrasill's ash. I give you Medusa and Stheno and Euryale. I give you the harpies and the witches, and the Fates . . . I give you Proserpine, the Queen of Hell. The five-and-ten-cent-store Lilith, the mother of Cain, the black widow who is poisonous and eats her mate.

This is a true witches' brew, but it is cooked up by men.

There are also male archetypes of death—the grim reaper, the skeleton. Perhaps it would be more accurate to say that they are neutral, because of their impersonal quality. They symbolize abstract mortality. But aging with its catalog of fleshly indignities is the human face of death, and it is a woman's face. There is no male counterpart to the witch or hag with her ugly features, warts, scrawny bones, and hanging flesh—nor any male figure who rivals the horror and loathing she inspires. She is the scapegoat par excellence for our fear of aging.

The image of the young beauty leaving Shangri-La who instantly shrivels into an aged hag and dies says it all. Much of the power of this image derives from its femaleness; this becomes clear if you try to replace it with a man.

Our traditional repositories of wisdom, then, give us a meager inheritance as women. We can take our pick from among shrews, bawds, neutered nobodies, and witches for models of aging. But this should not surprise us, since the arbiters of culture are, and have always been, male.

In our modern era the hag's power is attenuated. She mostly is cut down to the size of a *New Yorker* cartoon, or a cheap shot at the mother-in-law. No longer powerful, she is only ridiculous.

Fun at older women's expense is rampant in our culture. Question: How is it to be a grandfather? Answer: I like it but it's humiliating to be sleeping with a grandmother. *Playboy* features a full-page agist cartoon in every issue. This kind of fun is a one-way street: *Ms.* does not carry cuckold jokes or thigh-slappers about impotence. And a fifty-year-old wife does not talk about "trading in her aging husband for two twenty-five-year-olds."

The double standard of aging has its roots in our hallowed cultural tradition; this tradition sets the stage for what happens to women today. We were early made into symbols for aging—i.e., physical (and especially sexual) debilitation. Modern culture has made the denial of aging and the scapegoating of women for aging ever more efficient. The result is a society where it is acceptable for men, but not for women, to age.

3

MEN AND AGING

. . . I am hard. I wake up hard every morning, go to bed hard every night. I enjoy that. If you are not hard, you probably remember what it felt like when you were and wish you were again; if you are, you undoubtedly enjoy it as I do and want to stay that way.
FROM *Staying Hard* by Charles Gaines

Staying Hard

Men have big muscles, but in many ways they are the more vulnerable sex. To be male is to run a higher risk of death and disease from cradle to grave. Chromosomal structure gives women an edge. At all species levels, females—whether fruit flies, spiders, chickens, rats, or people—tend to live longer; as humans, four to ten years longer. Having two X chromosomes, instead of an X and a Y as do males, gives women several advantages. The double X cancels out harmful recessive mutant genes, and also controls resistance to disease.

The female hormones, estrogen and progesterone, are also protective. Studies indicate that estrogen helps women resist heart ailments. Progesterone, an anti-convulsive and sedative agent, may also work to increase women's survival capacity.

It is sometimes said, however, that the longevity gap is mainly due to the fact that women live less stressful lives. Whether we do or not, there is some evidence for women's constitutional superiority, all other things being equal. For example, in the fifties, a study was made of men and women in Benedictine monasteries who lived under a similar discipline. The women still outlived the men.

Men are also genitally vulnerable. The male body is relatively hard, lean, covered with a muscular sheath. The "soft underbelly," although a source of vulnerability, can be armored with muscle. But the genitals remain inescapably soft and accessible.

This physical structure shapes and also symbolizes the contradictions in the male experience. Men are expected to be tough, yet they are also vulnerable, in some ways more so than women. In fact, their most vulnerable part has been made the seat and symbol of their manhood. This paradox creates a central insecurity that men must constantly deal with. It is seldom discussed directly. But the vernacular clearly connects male vulnerability to genital structure: "to be had by the balls" is the quintessential male nightmare. And this equation of masculinity with toughness and sexual performance puts men in the position of being even more vulnerable than they would be simply on the basis of physiology. Strength vs. softness becomes their issue, one that colors their entire life, including their response to aging.

As men age, their sexual vulnerability increases. Their ability to achieve erection slows down appreciably in the forties, and in the elderly, full erection is often not attained until just before orgasm. Ejaculation is less frequent and less expulsive. However, there is a positive change as well; once erect, the older man can maintain this state for longer periods. And most men with a history of early and consistent sexual expression tend to remain sexually active in their later years.

The greatest bar to sexual expression in later life is not physiology but anxiety. Older men often withdraw from sex altogether; there is a dramatic decrease in lovemaking in later life which is not accounted for physiologically. So-called secondary impotence, that is, inability to achieve erection having no physical cause, is the major sexual problem of older men. Masters and Johnson found that 83 percent of all the men who experienced secondary impotence were over forty and of these, three out of four were over fifty. Especially striking was their finding that *every* male subject over forty expressed fears of impotence due to aging.

Again, this "phallic fallacy" has no organic basis, but it becomes a self-fulfilling hypothesis.

Staying Hard, the title of a popular exercise book, is the name of the male game. The hard penis is literally *de rigueur;* and preoccupation with penile size suggests an unconscious equation of the small penis with the castrated penis. But softness in any form can trigger unacceptable feelings of vulnerability—like the "bay window," the disclosure of emotion, or any of the changes that aging or illness can bring.

Staying hard is not an achievable goal, though for a while it may seem to be. After adolescence, men embark upon a long period of stability, just as women begin the upheavals of pregnancy and lactation. This experience predisposes men to think of their bodies as immutable. Men minimize their physical changes, while women exaggerate them. My uncle, no longer the slender fellow he used to be, will snort at "fat women who let themselves go"—unaware of his own creeping embonpoint. Masculine dress helps to minimize change in physique; suits tactfully cover a multitude of sins. Women, on the other hand, must often change their entire style as their measurements change because their clothing iṣ made to reveal. Men do not have these graphic reminders.

Thus the inevitable changes that aging or incapacity bring often come as a special shock to men. They had thought of their bodies as fixed and, having no context for accepting change, minimized its importance.

This pattern of toughing it out is bad for men's health. One study by Marjorie Lowenthal and others found that men who ran the highest risks were the stoics who denied their real health problems.

Women have also traditionally supported male denials of vulnerability. Early on, the idea of romance helps women to see men as invulnerable knights. Later, we discover that we ourselves are the real sustainers, but we pretend a lot to men to be weaker than we are. We are constantly advised to bolster their egos, to make *them* think that they are the strong ones. Our reasons for shoring them up are not totally disinterested, of course; we are largely dependent upon them economically. The result of this game is that women become unacknowledged but permanent crutches for men. We are expected to remain their support systems throughout our lives. But if, as we mature, we decide we have other fish to fry, this is experienced by men as a betrayal.

It then becomes a relatively simple matter to replace us with a younger, more supportive candidate. Most men are simply never required to deal with their own vulnerabilities. And if they have money or power, nothing else matters. A sociology professor told me, "When I see that row of smoothly tanned young honeys sitting there gazing adoringly at me it's an enormous turn-on, even though I know that it's only my role and that if I were Joe Shmoe walking along the street they wouldn't give me a second look. When I relate to my colleagues who are my peers, it somehow dilutes the sexual attraction." And Governor George Wallace, a middle-aged paraplegic, just married his third young wife. What if he were female?!

Men and Work

There is no room in the male cosmos for vulnerability, because male roles are economically defined. If women are sex objects in our culture, men are work objects. They have to be rocks, because rocks are predictable and always show up for work on time.

Rocks can be chipped into shape to fit particular niches in the work world. Work is not something that men do, but something they are. Witness our surnames: Mr. Cooper, Mr. Smith, Mr. Taylor, Mr. Fletcher—all names of occupations. Work is deeply synonymous with manhood.

Of course, women work too. In fact, 80 percent of women work. But as we have seen, the work role is usually not their major source of identity. Even though women often work at the lowest-status, most brutally dehumanizing jobs, they are not taught from infancy to *become* these jobs. Not yet, anyway.

Men jump into the work world with both feet because they're programmed for it—but also because it answers a felt need. The work world is controlled and controllable in a way that the vicissitudes of the body—especially in its sexual aspect—are not.

Rigid structures like job hierarchies, forty-hour work weeks, and bureaucratic regulations are reassuringly solid, stable, and unchanging. Besides, the work world rewards performance anxiety and the compulsiveness it engenders with promotions, prestige, and praise, while in the world of sexual and human relations it is a liability.

Socialization of males to the world of work starts in the cradle. Mothers and fathers praise boy babies for physical agility and strength. They are punished with disapproval for crying, and for being "too sensitive." They are expected to "perform." Little boys become chips off the old block; the jokes, games, and rituals of boyhood are the proving ground for male identity and become transposed into the work situation. By then, little room is left for softness.

It is true that men screw themselves by their own value system. But it is a system in which women also participate. For every swaggering macho, there is also a mother who taught him not to cry and a woman who bats her eyelashes adoringly at him. And although women may not be hung up on penis size, and may be understanding about episodes of impotence, they *do* want to be able to depend on "their" men. They want men in control. They want them to be successful. We complain about men's lack of expressiveness, but if they act vulnerable we often think they are wimps. And so we play a part in the creation of a no-win system which pressures men, while it holds us back.

The male work ethic evokes a list of words that all start with "p": profit, prestige, providing, performance, potency. The "p's" are the payoffs for keeping your nose to the grindstone, and are also the hallmarks of masculinity. Men are producers and providers; the paycheck is proof of potency. Sex and work are interchangeable both as symbol and substance of power.

Working gives men real satisfactions. The development of a life career offers a sense of self-definition, of challenge, of tangible and intangible rewards for effort. All this is hard for women to come by, even when they do work.

On the other hand, many men must work at jobs that give them some of these satisfactions but that also are trivial, boring, or harmful to people.

Men are trained not to pay too much attention to these aspects of the job. Tom Ucko, a career development consultant, told me, "A client I have right now is typical—he doesn't even notice how it feels to do the work itself. Now, these were tasks he himself had chosen as satisfying, but he meant the result. He didn't even *consider* how he feels . . . that's not an issue, that's not relevant."

The demands of the work role create an emotional straitjacket that men do not escape from easily. Years of working in emotionally neutral, power-oriented, and morally irrelevant slots have shaped them into cogs in the work machine. Marx called this condition "alienation."

An alienated man depends on the p-pay for satisfaction, instead of on more intrinsic sources of gratification. But at the very least, the work role defines men as valuable, productive members of society—and this definition is not challenged until they retire. Women, on the other hand, begin to feel the first intimations of expendability while still in their youth.

Women begin coping with "retirement" seriously around forty—and they often must do this with no support system to fall back on. Although the forties may also mark the onset of male jitters, it is not until sixty-five or so that men are phased into obsolescence. And retirement is a blow because they genuinely have something to lose: a privileged status that women have never known in the first place.

Retirement and Aging

"Loss of potency" is perhaps the most apt phrase to describe the male experience of aging. Because of the powerful tie-in of work, sex, and power, a blow in any one of these areas can affect the others. The first punch of aging often comes at the moment of some limiting event: perhaps an episode of impotence, perhaps some major physical disability, loss or impending loss of a job—sometimes when something happens to the spouse.

Death and disability are both more threatening and more immediate in the lives of men. Many are imprinted at midlife by the shocking death of one of their contemporaries; the first acquaintance or friend who suddenly keels over is likely to be male.

When men talk about aging, they mention limitations first. They might be concerned about getting bald or soft, but appearance is not the priority it is for women. It's function that counts. As one man said, "After cruising on the highway for years, all of a sudden I'm in crosstown traffic and the meter's running." For working men in particular, this physical slowdown may involve both a loss of self-esteem and real income. Retirement, of course, is the most threatening event of all. Worklessness means worthlessness to many. Ten percent of all workers face compulsory retirement, and 31 percent say that retirement is not their choice. According to Ken Dychtwald:

> Retirement . . . is a frightening process which kills or maims many men. They feel the impending ego-murder of themselves because they have overemphasized their professional identity. Because of the narrowness of this identification they have a hard time redefining their function. Their incapacity to tolerate weakness becomes their undoing because if they could ask for help they would not need it. . . . They knock themselves off rather than remain in a state of depression.

Male suicide statistics are a truly horrendous indication of male vulnerability. Although women attempt suicide four times as often as men, men actually succeed about three times as often as women. For all their difficulties, women clearly emerge as the survivors.

This survivability has to do with the flexibility women have been forced to develop. Men have a harder time adjusting to change. The female suicide curve is a plateau with a slight rise in the later forties which levels out again. The male curve is like the side of a mountain. Men start in their teens to kill themselves as often as women, and the curve climbs steadily, becoming ever steeper. Over sixty-five, their rate is five times higher than that of women. The rigidity of the male role is their undoing.

At retirement, men can theoretically seek new satisfactions

outside the marketplace that would transcend the usual "avocational" pursuits. Yet they get little cultural support for this. Since community service and non-paid work have traditionally been women's sphere, anything associated with them can be viewed as a drop in status and a further evidence of castration. Women can wear the pants, but the favor is not reciprocal.

One study found that many men talked in terms of making a broader social contribution, but when asked for details they talked about "taking the drudgery out of life," improving living standards—rather than a contribution that would take them out of the marketplace or at least reshape their ideas of what a contribution could be in a tangible form. The rat-race maze is narrow, and narrowing.

Women as Age Scapegoat

Accepting age and vulnerability, if you are male, means coming up with something better than "staying hard." Yet our system makes this very difficult. In order to deal with aging, men must reevaluate the myths they have lived by. For many, it is easier to find someone else to blame the problem on. And women fall readily to hand. It is just another facet of our "supportive" role.

The tradition of blaming women for the sufferings of men goes back a long way. Perhaps unconsciously men seek revenge for the pressures women have put on them throughout their lives. In any case, it would not surprise me if the goat that was heaped with all the woes of the Hebrews and driven into the desert was a nanny goat!

Women are scapegoated for males' declining potency. Women's sexual responsiveness changes little with age, yet they are the ones pegged with the onus of being asexual. Men's diminution of sexual interest is often laid at the door of their wives, who are considered to be no longer "attractive" enough to inspire their performance. Men rigged the game in their favor the minute they equated "sexiness" with the hallmarks of fertility—a definition that causes women to bear an unfair share of the stigma of aging.

These attitudes are so prevalent in our culture that even sex researchers share them. Masters and Johnson discuss aging changes in women at great length, constantly using loaded expressions like "steroid starvation," "estrogen deficiency," "seeming frigidity," and "unbalanced endocrine system in the postmenopausal years" to describe normal reductions of hormone levels that are no longer needed for reproduction. They then go on to trivialize women's activities by saying they are due to sexual frustration:

> Many members of this group [older women] demonstrate their basic insecurity by casting themselves unreservedly into their religion, the business world, volunteer social work, or over-zealous mothering of their maturing children and grandchildren. Deprived of normal sexual outlets, they exhaust themselves physically in conscious or unconscious effort to dissipate their accumulated and frequently unrecognized sexual tensions.

In discussing aging changes in men, the chapter has quite a different tone. No mention of steroid starvation appears, even though lowered male hormonal levels affect male sexual performance. Male activities and interests are not called into question. Instead, considerable space is devoted to "explanations" of male changes on a *non-hormonal* basis. The first one mentioned is sexual monotony (of course, the fault of the wives). The following passage is typical of the pseudoscientific style which thinly conceals their bias:

> The female partner in her forties may age, from the point of view of physical appearance, more rapidly than the male partner. Her overemphasis on or poor handling of the menopausal years may impart an aura of being "unfemale," with the result that she ceases to have a sexually stimulating cathexis.

Here we have the "men age better than women" myth in scientific dress. It is nowhere writ that the male jowls, potbelly, drooping testicles, or baldness are less ugly or old-looking because men have them. Yet we do not blame men for their "poor handling" of aging or tell them they are wrecking their "sexual cathexis" for us.

In the face of such putdowns, many women choose to put the lid on their sexuality. Sometimes they do it so as not to confront their aging husbands with their sexual needs. According to Lillian Rubin, "For most midlife women today, the needs and desires, frustrations and discontents, that men bring to the relationship still dictate [women's] behavior." Thus we get scapegoated into the role of has-been, and accept it so as not to threaten our mates.

The irony of this is that women at midlife are often feeling at least as sexual as before—and often more so. In fact, we have no way of knowing what the potential levels of older women's sexuality might be, given a more positive climate.

But our stance is to accept the prevailing hostile climate as a "given." We accept it to protect our men from the consequences of their own beliefs—beliefs that make aging and human vulnerability unacceptable. We are constantly reassuring them that they look fine, that they perform fine—or that we don't care that much anyway. Men do not reciprocate by reassuring *us*, but this does not discourage us. In fact we even buy the double standard of aging for ourselves. As one woman told me: "I like my husband's gray hair, I think it's distinguished. The weight he's gained doesn't bother me—no, I don't mind it at all. These things look fine on a man, but not on a woman."

This stance is disrespectful to men and injurious to ourselves. It treats men as incapable of genuinely coming to terms with aging. It implies that they need to be protected in their illusions by us. This discourages them from dealing creatively with their own problems. And in the name of a phony superiority it turns us into neutered mamas, instead of women who respect men enough to challenge them.

Teenage Boys and Middle-aged Moms

There is another source of male vulnerability which powerfully reinforces the double standard of aging. This is a psychosexual vulnerability stemming from the dynamics of the traditional nuclear family.

Psychologists have long pointed out the central conflict of growing up male in a nuclear family: mother is the first love, the nurturer, the source of loving body contact, the door to all tender feelings—yet this door must be closed if the boy is to become a man and bond with another woman. He starts to close it during boyhood, declining mom's caresses and ministrations of concern. He will be encouraged to participate in the "tough" male culture we have been examining, to eschew the female world altogether during a period of celibacy Freud called latency. The door stays closed until the pressure of adolescent sexuality forces it open again. But how dangerous it would be if mother still lurked behind the door! From her side, she must ease his passage by relating to him nonsexually. From his side, any residual attraction to her must be repressed now, so that he can transfer his erotic feelings to a girl his age. What better safeguard than to define mom as beyond the pale—she who had been the center of the universe is now seen as unimportant; she who had been the source of all erotic feeling is now seen as sexually unattractive. The family romance is over at puberty; mom becomes defined as matronly. The boy then is free to begin the mating game. He will eventually choose a wife, establish his own family.

But what will happen when his own children are teenagers, when his own wife reaches middle age? Perhaps the image of older woman as matron—uninteresting, sexless—still is enshrined in his psyche, a residue of his own adolescence. Perhaps he, too, will turn from his wife and reject her as his son may be doing. He may also seek a relationship with a younger woman. The "adolescent" quality of this search is striking and bewilders even the men who participate in it. The double standard of aging, then, may have important roots in the vulnerability of men to their mothers, particularly in our small nuclear families where mothers tend to focus inordinately upon their young children.

Women may collude in their own denigration within this family dynamic, out of unconscious concern for their sons' emancipation. By buying the matronly image of themselves, they reinforce the double standard of aging. They are right, of course, in sensing that the intensity of their sons' early attachment must be defused. But there are better ways to do this than by participating in their own subordination. Some of these might be: living in extended families, giving women gratifying opportunities outside the home, giving men a chance to nurture their children. But as things now stand, our system of family arrangements predisposes men to constantly cut women down to size. And the world of work they construct reinforces their inability to accept their vulnerabilities, and to use women as scapegoats for them instead.

Beyond Staying Hard

The men who successfully deal with aging are the ones who can expand their sense of self-worth beyond staying hard and the payoffs of prestige and performance. These men will likely have resolved their dependence upon mother that impels them to flee from all women-tainted activities. In *Working*, Studs Terkel quotes a sixty-two-year-old elevator operator talking about his piece of land in New Jersey. He evidently loves to cultivate it— and with it, his "feminine" side:

> Now my boys are building their places on it for their children. I run up there on Friday and get the place tidied up. When you get your corn, you never taste corn like that in the store. And you have your big red tomatoes come in and cabbage, and make sauerkraut. In the fall you can tomatoes and you can string beans and you make grape jelly and blackberry jelly. Now I put a pond in and I had fish put in, and now wild birds come.

Men who can accept their changing sexuality and their vulnerability are unlikely to scapegoat women to make themselves feel better. "My erectile capacity is damaged somewhat," reports a man of fifty-six. "For me, rediscovering my sexuality meant discovering it was not just in my penis, which actually feels a lot less restricting." These men who move beyond competition are unlikely to reject their older wives. Jack Cooper, a novelty manufacturer, told me:

> You get a view from the bridge with age. But I wasn't always so smart. It took my wife's cancer to change me. Now the rat race doesn't mean a thing to me. You realize how insignificant you are. It's too bad I had to gain a lot at my wife's expense, but we are happier now than when she was in perfect health. You don't have that pressure to conquer the world. I have lived all my life with a strange philosophy—the more I give the more I get coming back to me. I've shared all my life and because of that I keep mentally young and alert. You are surrounded by goodwill—the reward of virtue is the good life itself.

And Howard, a career counselor, says:

> The need for power "out there" is inversely related to feelings of powerfulness inside. Power "out there" keeps you from feeling scared. I realized this when I saw myself needing to beat my little kids at their children's board games—with shame and embarrassment! The more I could cope with feelings inside, the less I needed the trappings of power—that's what enabled me to break with the corporate world.

In one of his recent poems, "Fear and Trembling," Robert Penn Warren speaks of "Us who now know that only at death of ambition does the deep Energy crack crust, spurt forth, leap from grottoes, dark—and from the caverned enchainment."

When, he was asked, did ambition die for him?

> I would say in the forties. I was so wrapped up in the thing itself—the moment—that I had no sense of career. The process of writing became its own reward. I was forty-five or forty-six at the time; the pleasure in the thing itself comes fairly late. And that's where the energy comes from.

A young man's ambition to get along in the world and make a place for himself—half your life goes that way, till you're forty-five or fifty. Then, if you're lucky, you make terms with life, you get released.

As a woman looking at the crisis of male aging, I often feel that I am looking into Alice's mirror where everything is reversed. Women are deprived of opportunities for power; men are given a lethal overdose. Women are expected to lose their sexuality; men are expected to maintain it at peak levels indefinitely. Jack Sprat and his wife need to exchange some of the fat for some of the lean if both are to have a healthy diet.

As psychologist Daniel Levinson says:

When the work world is hypermasculine—when women are absent or highly subordinated, and many qualities in men are devalued as "feminine"—a man will find it harder to integrate the Masculine/Feminine polarity [in himself]. The freer participation of women in the work world is an important step towards the liberation of men from their one-sided masculinity. . . . Changes of this kind will also free women from the constraints imposed by the excessive feminization of parenting and by the discrimination that restricts their participation in most of our institutions.

The double standard of aging is a symptom of a system which locks both men and women into unsatisfying roles. It may give men a short-lived ego boost, but it helps to perpetuate a situation where everybody ultimately loses.

However, the reciprocity of our fates is also an augury of hope. Improvement in the lot of women will inexorably bring improvement in the lot of men, and vice versa. There is no way to deal with either sex's difficulties without everybody winning. All we have to do is change the rules of the game.

4

MIRROR, MIRROR: THE FEAR OF AGING

And when she had dressed herself in beautiful clothes she went to her looking glass and said, "Mirror, mirror, on the wall, who is fairest of them all?" The looking glass answered, "O queen, although you are of beauty rare, the young bride is a thousand times more fair." Then she railed and cursed and was beside herself with disappointment and anger.

Grimm's Household Stories

Appearance Anxiety

Being older is a problem for both men and women, but *looking* older is women's special problem. Men do not turn into pumpkins at the stroke of midlife; only women become nonpersons as a result of appearance changes. Thus, women have a special fear of aging I shall call "appearance anxiety."

Appearance anxiety in women is comparable to performance anxiety in men. The different kinds of anxiety we manifest are due to the difference in our roles. As de Beauvoir pointed out: "The mature man is involved in enterprises more important than those of love; and since in him the passive qualities of an object are not called for, the changes in his face and body do not destroy his attractiveness . . . woman, on the contrary, is allowed no hold on the world save through the mediation of some man."

Women often can accept the diminished functioning that age brings more philosophically than men can. But losing our looks often triggers deep, irrational feelings of losing everything. This anxiety is considered normal in women, and the entire beauty industry is based upon it.

Appearance anxiety may be our special problem, but the emphasis on appearance is not just in ourselves, but everywhere. Looks have always mattered, but never so much as today. Our entire culture is on the make, and so we are obsessed with keeping up appearances. The image is what counts. Image-making is a respected profession. If the image is right, the reality doesn't matter; the image *is* the reality. Tell a corporation that its behavior is unethical; it merely smiles a corporate smile. But tell it that its behavior is adversely affecting its image! That is another story.

Women are especially in bondage to mirrors—the real kind, and the kind that are in people's eyes. We are told this is narcissism, but we know that it is a form of survival. All powerless groups need the approval of those in power. Mirrors are to image what scales are to weight: a measurement of our acceptability, or even of our reality.

I *saw* myself in the mirror for the first time at the age of five. Of course, I had *looked* in the mirror before, but suddenly my reflection conveyed the enormously exciting idea: "This is me." That moment was the beginning of my self-awareness. Many women continue to verify their existence throughout their lives by looking in mirrors.

Women look *for* themselves in mirrors; men don't. Men look *at* themselves: Do I need a shave? Is my hair combed? "When I look in the mirror I just give a quick glance and walk away," they say.

Women approach mirrors like lovers. They prepare to "be seen" by themselves, subconsciously choosing certain angles, certain expressions. Catching oneself unawares in a street mirror can throw women into confusion: they do not "know" the person whose unfamiliar shape or way of moving they have just inadvertently glimpsed.

Women are looked at but not truly *seen*. Glances bounce off our surface as reflections bounce off mirrors, and we live with this sense of being constantly viewed and evaluated. For some of us, the surface is a shield. For others, it is a prison. Nevertheless, our knowledge that we live under observation makes us self-conscious, and colors our behavior. Our movements have a studied quality. We toss our hair, smooth down our skirts, cross our legs, smile. We know we are being looked at. We may yawn prettily, but never pick our teeth, scratch ourselves, belch. That kind of spontaneous movement is reserved for men.

Women from cultures not dominated by mirrors have an unselfconscious beauty that one almost never sees here. I once waited for a bus next to a classically beautiful Mexican peasant woman. Never once did an expression cross her face that was for the benefit of another person. Even my impertinent scrutiny left her unmoved; she was not programmed to be aware of herself as image.

From childhood we are trained in the importance of looks; the good girl in fairy tales is always the pretty one. Mothers, with a sharp eye on the marriage market, put their daughters on diets, straighten teeth, give ballet lessons, fix noses. Our magazines teach us to know our "good points" and our "figure flaws." Mirrors are our constant companions—and our companions are our constant mirrors: "Yecch, my hair looks awful, doesn't it?" "Gee, you look great. You look as if you've lost about seven pounds." *About* seven pounds. This obsessive monitoring of our bodies is as much a part of our life as brushing our teeth. Surface and contour are scrutinized; a small varicosity is a repulsive red spider, an age spot is always horrid, and to all of us incipient (or clinical) anorexics, fat is the most revolting thing possible. We are taught early: How we look is who we are. Youth and beauty are considered synonyms; we don't even have expressions for looking good without looking younger. When we look lousy, we say, "I feel like I look 110." The biggest gun is always age.

Our early reliance on mirrors sets the stage for the fear of aging. Although most women I spoke to would nod affirmatively if I asked if they accepted their age and appearance, if I asked, "When you look in the mirror, what do you feel?" a shadow would cross their faces and they would hesitate. The most vulnerable position for an aging woman is facing the mirror. This is true for women wearing Paris originals, jeans, polyester pant suits, for Europeans as well as Americans.

Our appearance anxiety is our big secret. As older women, we will readily discuss most problems such as our health, our finances—legitimate concerns that are shared by most of us. But the looks issue touches sources of pain that seem too personal to share. To admit to our appearance anxiety means to publicly acknowledge uncomfortable feelings: our feelings of having failed as women. It also means admitting to our membership in the great underclass of "Women Men Do Not Value." Admitting all this is a further blow to our pride.

The silence and shame surrounding women's aging prevails even within the family. Our mothers probably prepared us for menstruation, but how many talked to us about menopause or aging? Most of the current books on mothers and daughters do not even mention this important issue. We go forward into this realm of experience with as little preparation as did Victorian women for menstruation.

Because of this silence, we think we are alone in our anxieties. We are ashamed of ourselves; we can't conceive of the other sensible women we know "freaking out" over such a superficial thing as looks. But we are not alone. Appearance anxiety is as much a social reality as our low income. Our shame leads us to pretend casualness, but we spend $8 billion a year on the fountain-of-youth cosmetics market. The prices we are willing to pay there are a truer measure of our real feelings.

Some women did discuss their relationship to mirrors quite frankly:

I look at myself a lot. Mostly I look at myself and feel good, especially when the lights are dim. I see lines coming out and I'm very conscious of them . . . in bright light I feel uneasy and self-conscious. I don't mind *being* older, I just don't want to *look* older. Being forty is not glorious—but this is a product of the time.

My looks are catching up with me. Three years ago I looked in the mirror and said, "You will never look better in your life." I noticed that change of verb.

How we catalog our defects!

There are times when I look at myself intensely with or without clothes on, especially when I feel like I'm changing shape . . . I don't like it when I'm fatter or when my hair looks yucky.

When I look in the mirror I see the wrinkles between my brows here. No, this is not the sort of face I want for myself.

I try not to make a big deal of it, but when I look in the mirror I notice the little things that are shouting to the world, "You are getting older!" I don't like this loose skin under my chin.

Men as Our Mirrors

In our obsession with image, the eyes of others are ultimate mirrors. And the significant others are the people whose opinions carry weight for us. I quote from "Dulse," a short story by Alice Munroe:

I had noticed something about myself on this trip to the Maritimes. It was that people were no longer so interested in getting to know me. *By people I mean men.* I don't mean that I created a stir before, but something was there that I could rely on. I am forty-five, I haven't gotten thinner or fatter and my looks have not deteriorated in any alarming way, but nevertheless I had stopped being one sort of woman and had become another.

By "people," we generally do mean men. They are the significant others par excellence—the race of mankind for which we are the means of production, the makers of history, assigners of value, creators of culture, purveyors of opportunity, dispensers of security. To make men unimportant is to choose a life marginal to the mainstream of human existence. To be seen as unimportant to men is—with few exceptions—not to be seen at all. It is that simple.

Women, children, and dogs can love us, but only men can give us *recognition* because of the clout that they wield. Women can love men, but even men need the recognition of other men to be truly visible.

The need for recognition is universal; it is not a weakness. Eric Berne conceives of this "recognition-hunger" as "a partial transformation of infantile stimulus-hunger," that is, of the baby's need to be physically stimulated in order to survive. "After the period of close intimacy with the mother is over, the individual . . . under most conditions will compromise. He learns to do with more subtle, even symbolic forms of handling, until the merest nod of recognition may serve the purpose to some extent."

By the time we are adults, there are "different strokes for different folks"—or, as Berne says: "A movie actor may require hundreds of strokes each week from anonymous and undifferentiated admirers, while a scientist may keep physically and mentally healthy on one stroke a year from a respected master." What we all have in common is the need for stroking from those we define as the significant others in our world.

Deprive a woman of recognition by those who matter to her and she dies a little. Even our everyday speech acknowledges this connection between attention and survival: when we ignore someone, we "cut them dead."

Men receive strokes for what they do in the world, and in addition, when they come home, they get stroked by their wives. Part of a woman's job is to give strokes to men. Researcher Pam Fishman placed tape recorders in people's homes and found that women punctuate life with conversational invitations to men. She called this role of women in everyday talk "conversational shitwork."

When men need strokes on the job and at home, this is called a normal need for recognition. When women need strokes, this is called dependency. The real difference between men and women is not the *need* for strokes but the *amount received*. This is particularly true at midlife. Our dependency on recognition from men leads us to adopt their criteria for aging, instead of finding our own. We are supersensitive to the messages they give us, and we accept their evaluations with little resistance.

Thus, we usually don't discover that we are getting old from internal cues; our first messages are liable to come from the outside. We feel no real diminution of capability, strength, or sexuality, but we are simply put into another category by the eyes of others. What these eyes tell us is that they will no longer mirror us. The eyes make no contact; they glance and slide off as if they had seen an inanimate object. Like the victims of Count Dracula, we look in the mirror but get no reflection back. The bite on the neck signifying male approval introduces a time-release poison: it is a bleach; we fade gradually; we become invisible.

Some women told me candidly that they felt older not because of any intrinsic change, but because of this shift in the quality and amount of attention they were getting:

The first time I felt a twinge was when I queued up for an ice cream and the man behind the counter gave my turn to a young pretty girl. I remember thinking, so that's what it's like. He just didn't see me.

A boy of twenty-five will not look at you in the same way as at a girl of twenty-five.

As a kid I was always fascinated by the articles in women's magazines showing diagrams of face shapes and giving instructions how you "should" wear and apply makeup. I wanted to conform and do the right thing but I felt like a dummy because I could never figure out if my face was round, oval, square, or heart-shaped. Now that I'm in my menopause, I'm not even addressed with the "shoulds," I'm ignored.

I remember when I was younger, older people were invisible to me. Two older friends of my parents had an affair. The thought of them in bed together was so ludicrous—and to think that they were ten years younger than I am now!

I had large breasts and when I walked down the street the men would "come on" to me, and even though I thought at the time that I was irritated by this, I must admit that I miss my youth a little.

A retired madam, at forty, says:

The older a woman gets, the less distinguished she gets. Men are really attracted to young, beautiful women, and you miss the seductive remarks. Yet they always notice your voice, your intelligence, the things that only come with age. You have to work harder to be more attractive.

We learn that age is a liability. A high school teacher, fifty-nine, relates:

A group of us were having a discussion about how old we feel in spirit. Others said thirty-two, nineteen . . . I said fifty, and there was this great gasp. I just feel like I'm a different person now, and that's the age I feel. But it was as if I had said something awful, that my response was in some way embarrassing. I won't say that again!

The California counterculture provides no immunity. "I used to jump into the hot tub and think nothing of it," a forty-year-old told me. "But suddenly last year at a conference I found myself self-conscious when I took off my clothes: I was somewhat reluctant to let it all hang out. I *did* get into the hot tub but I stayed under the water line!"

The shift of status is abrupt and unmistakable. That youth is valued and age is not is made clear in millions of ways, some subtle, some not. But women get the message. Ani Mander, a writer and professor, comments:

There is a certain leeway until forty. At forty you are over the hill—as far as they perceive you. When they can no longer dominate you, you are considered over the hill.

A homemaker:

What makes you think you're not young is the way people look at you. Some days when you are feeling pessimistic you say, "My commercial value is getting weaker."

A secretary, sixty-one:

It becomes a chore to remain beautiful but I do undertake it. I take care of my skin as best I can, I sew my clothes. It's important to be as presentable as possible. I use Loving Care, otherwise my hair would be white. White-haired people have a struggle, especially in the business world, and I work in the business world.

And in case you miss the nonverbal messages, there are always the forms of address to remind you that you are in another category:

"It's that moment when they start to call you 'madam' instead of 'miss.' Even when it's nicely done, you feel the difference."

"I gradually slid from *jeune fille* to *femme* after my children grew up."

A black woman: "Instead of 'Hi, baby,' I now get 'Hello, lady.'"

Since being defined as old has nothing to do with real aging, you can be considered over the hill at any arbitrarily chosen age. In some circles it is thirty or thirty-five or twenty-one. Beth Trier, the *San Francisco Chronicle*'s fashion editor, mentioned to designer Perry Ellis that someone she worked with was a great fan of his. Ellis asked the woman's age, and when Trier said thirty-five, he sniffed, "She's a little old to be wearing my clothes." And Rita Jenrette's husband told her, "Why would *Playboy* use a thirty-one-year-old when they can get all the eighteen-year-olds they want?" Why indeed?

The following comments by Frances Lear pose the question: How different is L.A. from real life?

Los Angeles is no place for a woman. Out here, a woman is a nonperson unless she is under twenty-one, powerful, or a star. In this quid-pro-quo town, the flip side of an aging female without box-office clout or her own daily newspaper is an aging man, without the power to hand out parts, out on a date with an actress.

But men benefit from a double standard that covers the city like a shroud, enabling them to grow old gracefully because the aging process for men is more often concurrent with the build-up of power. In screeching contrast, aging women are dismissed as "over the hill." The hill ends in late pubescence.

Since men are our mirrors, we seldom see beauty in age and are outspoken about our distaste for looking old.

When I was young, I saw women over forty all around me. They seemed so *old*. I rejected that image of the traditional older woman and I still do.

I am afraid of being classed as a *vieille dame* [old woman], that young people will look at me the way I looked at older people—that is to say, I spoke politely but they didn't interest me. For example, in a group the young people will call others by their first name, and to me say *madame* or *vous* instead of *tu*.

I am afraid. I was very happy to be thirty, but not forty. If I look younger it will be OK to be forty, but if I don't look younger, I'll be upset if people don't say, "Wow, you look younger!" I take more care of my appearance now. I run to the hairdresser—I can't stand my gray hair showing—and I dress in black because I feel my breasts are too fat, and no more pants. And I don't wear short sleeves—I think of my grandmother's arms with the flesh hanging down. Ugh! And I think, "Do I look like that?"

A natural corollary of this distaste for our own bodies is our ambivalence about telling our age. Many women I spoke with will do so, but few do so simply and naturally.

I always tell my age because if I say I'm thirty they would think I'm old-looking—and that would not be very intelligent. But if I say I'm fifty-one the people think, Oh, she looks good!

I always hated to tell my age because I never looked it. If I have the choice I don't tell—I say, "I'm not what you think." But I don't lie exactly. If I'm asked exactly my age I feel it's too intrusive.

I am afraid of dating references . . . shall I tell people I went to my twenty-fifth reunion? Yet I want credit for my experience too.

I heard a saying once: "A woman that will tell her age will tell anything." I don't actually lie, but I don't readily tell.

Aging, like life, is a continuum. But few women experience it this way. Since our view of our own aging is male-defined, we overemphasize the fertile years. Although this fertile period is roughly only one-third of a woman's life, it so defines us that we even exaggerate its length.

There are definite stages of life—childhood, adolescence, *then the longest and most fruitful* [italics mine]. And then, suddenly, I don't know if you'd call it old age, but a change, and it's physical in the sense of ills that you never expected.

But some women are able to see the fertile years as only one part of the continuum. This perspective is more related to role than nationality. A traditional French farm wife explained it this way:

Until puberty, one is a child, then one is an adolescent. Adulthood usually means marriage and family. Then at age forty-five to sixty-five, one is at the age of reason, reflection. Sixty-five marks the edge of retirement and old age. All the ages are good in their own ways—each slice of life has its purpose.

When I told Tillie Olsen my age, fifty-one, she said, "Just a baby." Her comment showed me the years of learning I still had ahead of me.

Appearance Anxiety Denial

Like any fear, we may first deal with aging by denial. And the silence and shame surrounding aging are both cause and consequence of this denial. As young women, we find it possible to believe we will not age, or believe that we can avoid its consequences. Jane, twenty-one, who works in a grocery store, told me: "I'm not worried about aging. I'll exercise, and I'll take care of my body. I'll use Rachel Perry" (a line of currently fashionable creams). I had the impression that she genuinely believed she could forestall all signs of age by means of the magical jars.

Denial keeps us from envisaging our future. Our pictures of ourselves as we age are usually dim or nonexistent. In my workshops, I often ask people to imagine themselves at ten-year intervals. The images tend to fall away around forty, and the exercise is resisted. Others who work with aging issues report the same phenomenon.

Sometimes women become aware of their denial: "I forget I

have gray hair," one of them told me. "Then, when I pass a mirror, I'm surprised to see it." And an actress said: "The young really see your age, and sometimes you don't realize it yourself. When my director asked me to play the role of a mother in a play, I was shocked."

Some women maintain their denial—and covertly ask others to support it: "I'm seventy-one," she said, pausing for the expected "My, but you certainly don't look it" retort. She did. Women everywhere who, to my eyes, looked every year of their age told me that they of course were aware of looking younger.

We have all seen the women like my Mrs. Miller of the beauty salon—the grotesquely embalmed older women whose presentation is pathetically out of keeping with their age. Talking to another "Mrs. Miller" in a café, I asked her how she felt when she looked in the mirror. She replied, "When I look in the mirror, well, I must say that when I wear a hat I feel better. I think women who don't wear hats are very foolish to give them up; men look at women with hats on. I do feel strongly about that." (She was wearing a pink hat, with pink shoes, purse, and pants suit.)

Surely another manifestation of denial is the discrepancy between many women's actual age and the age they feel "inside." Usually their internal age falls within the "fertile zone." This is due in part to the fact that the images we formed of older women no longer correspond to modern realities. But it also must be due to the fact that we deny our age; even in our imagination we hang on to youth: "In my head, age fifty is fatter than me, with a quality a bit like a grandmother—it doesn't match me at all."

Appearance Anxiety and the Life Span

Fear of aging starts young. I was surprised to find that it can set in shortly after adolescence. Feminist Zoe Moss writes:

My daughter is a senior in college. She already talks about her "youth" with a sad nostalgia. She is worried because she is not married. . . . Everything confirms in her a sense of time passing, that she will be left behind, unsold on the shelf. She already peers in the mirror for wrinkles and buys creams and jellies to rub into her skin. Her fear angers me but leaves me helpless. . . . I want to beg her not to begin worrying, not to let in the dreadful dull gnawing already.

Because of the exaggerated importance given to the years of fertility, the "movable doom" that haunts women's lives, as Susan Sontag called it, commonly descends in the thirties: "My thirtieth birthday was hard for me. I started thinking I'm over the peak, 'it's all downhill from here' sort of stuff. I got really depressed. I went out and bought forty dollars' worth of creams. Stupid, huh?"

Jane, fifty-five, recalled: "After the birth of my second child at thirty, I got my first tiny eye wrinkle and varicose vein and was mortified to be seen in a bathing suit. I ran right out to buy some stuff to cover it. I thought, 'Well, life is pretty much over for me.' I was unhappily married and thought, 'Well, this is it.' "

This reaction to such seemingly minor changes is understandable. That first "nothing" wrinkle breaks through the denial of aging. It initiates the long process of letting go of youth and coming to terms with aging. This process is a normal part of maturing, but in our society we approach it kicking and screaming. That first wrinkle tells us that the loss of youth *will happen to us*—but the gains that maturity will bring remain nebulous or nonexistent in our minds.

In her novel *The Vagabond*, Colette expresses this feeling of impending doom:

> My lover offers me his life, the improvident and generous life of a young man of about thirty-four, like me. He thinks I am young, too, and does not see the *end*—my end. In his blindness he will not admit that I must change and grow old, although every second, added to the second that is fleeting, is already snatching me away from him.

Appearance anxiety seems to peak in early midlife. Around forty, the image of being a "young woman" finally shatters for good. Sometimes the mirror conveys the message. Allison Lurie, in *The War Between the Tates,* superbly documents this process:

> Erica crosses the room to her dressing table, sits down, and looks into the glass, smiling slightly. For forty years she has had a happy relationship with mirrors. . . .
>
> Now, on this cold March night, Erica sits and for the first time in weeks looks close into it, smiling gently, anticipatively. A woman whom she scarcely recognizes looks back at her, first with a blank, then with an injured and startled expression. This person is whey-faced, middle-aged and skinny, with a hollow goose-flesh chest above her ill-fitting, inappropriately girlish dress. Her dark hair has been chopped off too short above a too-long neck, and what remains shows crinkled threads of gray. The stranger's nose is pinched, her mouth tight. Only the eyes—large, gray, thick-lashed—are familiar to Erica, and now they blink and turn in nets of tiny wrinkles, like caught fish.

Later, one becomes more accepting—or resigned:

> One gets older gradually, from day to day. Nature is well designed that way—if that happened overnight it would be horrible! Forty-five was hard—to lose my youth—but in spite of my wrinkles I know how to maintain my vitality. At fifty I learned to accept all that—one sees all that will no longer be, but one is calmer, more accepting.

Nevertheless, distaste for the "old lady" image can persist into old age. A therapist of eighty-three confessed:

> You'd think at my age I'd be less concerned about my looks, but no! I never was really beautiful but I always looked reasonably decent and enjoyed dressing well. The effect was that I could get by reasonably well. There was a long period there—fifty, sixty, seventy—when the beauties didn't look all that different from me—I liked that! But now I know that

whatever I do, I can't help seeing this exhausted-looking face, hair drooping down—I just don't like it!

And a musician, seventy-nine: "I am somewhat afraid of aging. I try to be young because it's sad to look white-haired and old. I color my hair. I don't like to dress in sad things, I like colors!"

Aging is not easy to accept for anybody. But the task is made doubly difficult for women because our culture refuses to see it as a natural process that happens to everybody. Women are made to feel ashamed that they age, and those that age less quickly are made to feel superior to those who don't. (I remember similar social norms about pregnancy: to look "less pregnant" was always a mark of superiority.) In this way, the double standard reinforces our denial of aging.

The Hall of Mirrors

Our mirrors are the eyes of the powerful, those we need and depend on. Women have had to train themselves to be sensitive to behavioral cues coming from the dominant (male) culture. But to base one's identity on these cues is like trying to find out who you are in a hall of mirrors. This exteriorization of our identity makes us enormously vulnerable. An admiring glance or compliment may cheer us today, but a lack of response may plunge us into depression tomorrow. And even the best mirror is only two-dimensional; it can never give us any solidity. Joan's description of her fortieth birthday is like a seesaw:

I hate being invisible to anyone male under thirty. In a workshop at Esalen on my fortieth birthday I was told it must be my twenty-seventh. What a present! But later, in an encounter group where you have to be honest, a guy said, 'Well, you're certainly under sixty, and not more than forty-five!' That nearly killed me. But *then* he said, 'I say that because you are the *oldest* woman I ever was sexually attracted to'! Of course that redeemed him; I loved it.

Trying to find out who you are by means of your reflection in a mirror is literally a vain proposition. Thus many women, confused about their looks, are also confused about who they are. Having no internal basis for our judgments about our looks leaves us rudderless. Rose Godina, a cosmetologist, says: "When one no longer knows what one's face is, one no longer knows who one is."

Not knowing how we look sometimes plunges us into agonies of indecisiveness. An Englishwoman had an apt phrase for it: "I find myself walking through department stores not knowing what to buy. I have a horror of looking like 'mutton dressed as lamb,' if you know what I mean."

Because we are dealing with reflections and not substance, our judgments lack objectivity. We often perceive incorrectly, like Erica in *The War Between the Tates*, alternately flattering ourselves and belittling ourselves.

For women who have been especially dependent on society's mirrors, aging is especially difficult.

I was extraordinarily pretty. I went through a period when I felt worse about all this than now. I couldn't accept that the romantic era was gone. I remember sitting by the phone hoping someone would call, and many of my friends who were also unable to solve the problem would call!

Somewhere within ourselves, however, we sense what is being done to us. We know that there is something wrong about our bondage to male values—even though we may acquiesce in it. Women everywhere voiced their resentment about the unfairness and arbitrariness of the double standard of aging.

I think the double standard is terrible. There are so many lonely old women, and the fact that women outlive men makes it worse. I've gone on two cruises—and never again! They are about seventy-five percent middle-aged women looking for a little romance.

People think it's perfectly OK for Prince Charles to be thirty-two and Lady Diana nineteen—that's wonderful! But if the ages were reversed there'd be a terrible big flap about it . . . yet she'll probably outlive him.

I'm flattered if people say I don't look my age but also angered about that emphasis. *Why do we have to look young?*

At the very least, women often feel ambivalence about their complicity:

I am ambivalent about the time-consumingness of this whole business of looks for women. It is difficult for me to outgrow my vanity because it is a source of pleasure for Fred. I'd love to cut my hair short, but he really likes long hair on me.

A woman of fifty must make an enormous effort to be accepted by the young. When one is thirty everything is excused by the freshness of youth, but at fifty one needs intelligence and good physical condition. Sometimes I just feel like letting it all go—it's too difficult.

Beyond Mirrors

Many of us do learn to move beyond mirrors. And some lucky ones among us never were reared to base their identities on reflections. These women, because of their personal histories, their social milieus, or their extraordinary achievements, have been able to take hold of the world without depending on looks.

Women who early decided that they did not have the physical equipment to play the looks game have already made their adjustments, for better or worse; appearance changes do not carry the same terror for them. If anything, they are now on a more equal social footing with their formerly "attractive" sisters. "A beautiful woman," writes Simone Weil, "looking at her image in the mirror may very well believe the image is herself. An ugly woman knows it is not."

Certain social milieus put less stock in appearance. Working-class women in both Europe and America are less "romantic." They deny less. Having fewer illusions about life leads to less disillusion later. And women who live traditional life styles that have not been shattered by widowhood, divorce, or economic insecurity often find compensation for the aging process.

These are the best of times for me. My six kids are finally launched, and frankly, I just enjoy being home and being able to do what I want. I think maybe I'm lazy! But I honestly don't feel any great need to do something else.

But even for women such as this, *the* fear is that they will end their lives discarded or widowed, becoming helpless or dependent upon children. These fears of solitude in old age are of course well founded. The gender arrangements of our culture stack the cards against a peaceful acceptance of aging for women.

For black women, the looks issue is enormously important, but it appears to be related more to racism than to agism:

The deep psychological trauma of growing up in a society that does not mirror you affects all black women. We have a terrible time over the issue of our looks, the lightness of our skin, our hair. It's terrible! Even darker babies don't get adopted.

And on aging:

In the black community, if you've got a good pair of legs, a strong behind, even if you're eighty you're OK. And you can't ever be *too* big; the model type just doesn't go.

Rural women are less dependent on youthful looks; rural values are embedded in firmer stuff than images. Life after youth goes on much as before. Children and grandchildren come and go, tasks may change but usefulness continues. Older people in the community and family remain valuable as persons in their own right and as role models.

Mme. B. lives on a Normandy farm without a TV. The morning we talked, she wore a large rubber apron over her unstylish dress because she was making a pâté. She finds the contemporary attitude toward looks perplexing:

When I was young, the important thing was to be healthy. Tuberculosis was the big fear, so girls that were well built and not too thin were considered pretty. Now everyone wants to lose weight. It is nice to look young, but what is the point of a youthful face if you puff going up stairs? Or lifted cheeks with sagging arms?

Mrs. Corcoran lives in a small town where she and her husband take in guests and have a garden. She chatted with me over a cup of tea.

There's something wrong if you can't fill up each age. I took care of an old woman of eighty-three. "I'd just as soon be on my way," she said to me. Now there's something wrong with that. My children say, why don't you tint your hair, but there's nothing so silly as a woman trying to look younger than she is. Each stage has a different behavior. I'd like to be seen as sensible. That jazzy stuff is not for a woman my age. A face lift? No way! If I had a lot of money I'd like to take a nice vacation someplace.

We sometimes feel nostalgia for this traditional way of living and aging. Mary, an extremely attractive fifty-five-year-old, is married to an international executive. Her beautifully styled hair is gray, and her body gives evidence of care and regular exercise. She made the following comment upon hearing that I was writing about women and aging: "I have an image of a red-cheeked, roly-poly grandma who looks like a real grandma. Look at me!" she said wistfully, indicating her stylish dress. "I'm a grandma too, but all I have is the gray hair." I sensed her longing for permission to grow old naturally.

In the lesbian community, age is no drawback. On the contrary, older women are sought after. "We had a group called, with tongue in cheek, 'Slightly Older Lesbians,' " the author Susan Griffin told me. "We met not because we felt rejected but because the younger women were too callow. We were considered, if anything, more attractive than younger women. For example, a woman of sixty-five in this group told me that many younger women made declarations of love to her. But lesbian women still go through fears of aging anyway—we also have to get jobs, shop at the Safeway. In other words, we deal with the same social milieu." (In the male homosexual community, however, being older is a terrible disadvantage, because being homosexual does nothing to change the male system that equates attractiveness with youth.)

Some women are raised in exceptional circumstances that insulate them from our cultural biases. Independence helps to diffuse the youth hangup, be it financial or professional. A French Literature professor told me: "My father was a doctor and he always encouraged me to use my mind; it never occurred to me that there was anything I couldn't do because I was a woman. I never was a 'coquette,' I never worried about how I looked." And Tillie Olsen writes in *Silences:*

> Fortunate are those of us who are daughters born into knowledgeable, ambitious families where no sons were born; fortunate are those in economic circumstances beyond the basic imperatives, thus affording some choice; fortunate are those in whose lives is another human being "protecting and stimulating the health of highest productivity"; fortunate are those of us to whom encouragement, approval come at the foundering time before it is too late . . . fortunate are those who live where relationships, opportunities not everywhere available are.

And Frances Lear writes: "Prejudice toward aging vanishes if a woman is a legend. No one counts birthdays when the Chief Justice of California, Rose Bird, comes to tea, or Sue Mengers, the superagent, or the 20th Century–Fox production chief, Sherry

Lansing. Like other women of extreme accomplishment, they are ageless—and sought after."

But no woman, however accomplished, is by definition invulnerable. Simone de Beauvoir felt the same pressures upon her that touch all women:

I thought, one day when I was forty: "Deep in that looking glass, old age is watching and waiting for me; and it's inevitable, one day she'll get me." She's got me now. I often stop, flabbergasted, at the sight of this incredible thing that serves me as a face. I understand La Castiglione, who had every mirror smashed. I had the impression once of caring very little what sort of figure I cut. In much the same way, people who enjoy good health and always have enough to eat never give their stomachs a thought. While I was able to look at my face without displeasure I gave it no thought, it could look after itself. The wheel eventually stops. I loathe my appearance now: the eyebrows slipping down toward the eyes, the bags underneath, the excessive fullness of the cheeks, and that air of sadness around the mouth that wrinkles always bring. Perhaps the people I pass in the street see merely a woman in her fifties who simply looks her age, no more, no less. But when I look, I see my face as it was, attacked by the pox of time for which there is no cure.

De Beauvoir, with her characteristic eloquence and honesty, breaks the taboo against discussing appearance anxiety. Yet how sad her words are—sadder still when we realize that she was a beautiful woman when she wrote them.

5

NEUTERING

Pray, sisters,
That the giant bird who eats our heart
Will raise his wings and go.
Pray for our treacherous soul.
Pray that the fire of love
Will leave our loins
The seed wither
The living blood subside.
                    Leah Alexander

The Myth of Neutering

Making women invisible is a good trick. The Lady Vanishes, and the sleight of hand is subtle, hard to see. It is also hard to talk about, because the words to describe it simply don't exist. As I wondered how to make the invisible visible, the two words which came first to my mind were *emasculation* and *castration*. They are wonderful words, loaded with nuance of damage above and beyond the genital. Say *castration* or *emasculation* and you trigger a host of images—and you also marshal immediate sympathy for the victim.

But these words are in the male domain. One cannot say a woman is castrated or emasculated. And subtly this implies that we do not have a potency that can be taken away. This linguistic second-class status is the unkindest cut of all. There is no sex-blind word in our language for the taking away of a person's force and effectiveness. For lack of a better word, I'll call it neutering.

Neutering is one of the principal ways the double standard of aging is enforced. It is based on the lethal myth that women undergo a physiological change which renders them sexless and at the same time worthless. It is held to be the normal state for older women.

Men can be neutral, but women can only be neutered. Neutral means unrelated to sex; neutered means desexed. Men can shift into neutral because they are not solely defined in terms of sex. Women, on the other hand, are viewed as either "having it" or "not having it." Standard male clothing is not perceived as neutering, but merely as neutral. A business suit and comfortable shoes can even be seen as enhancing a man's sexuality. A woman who wears a similar outfit is read as unfeminine or neutered. Women must steer between the Scylla of looking "too sexy" and the Charybdis of appearing desexed. "Dress for success" books and courses help women to navigate this perilous course to professional acceptability: gray for sobriety, skirts to show we're not trying to "wear the pants," heels and stockings to reveal "just enough" leg, but neatly trimmed hair so as not to give the impression of wild abandon, etc. Still, these outfits seem somehow a bit stiff and artificial; this is because the neutral modality which they are trying to create simply does not exist for women.

A priest can be celibate and wear black; he is neutral but retains his sexual identity. A nun, on the other hand, is more readily put into the category of a neutered woman who is assumed to have no sexual feelings. Madonna and whore are still our choices—until middle age, when we no longer are given the choice.

Neutering is a social process, but it is blamed on physiological changes. Freud unanalytically supported this common notion in an article on obsessional neurosis written in 1913:

> It is well known, and has been a matter for much complaint, that women often alter strangely in character after they have abandoned their genital functions. They become quarrelsome, peevish, and argumentative, petty and miserly; in fact,

they display sadistic and anal-erotic traits which were not theirs in the era of womanliness. Writers of comedy and satirists have in all ages launched their invective against the "old termagant" into which the sweet maiden, the loving woman, the tender mother, has deteriorated.

David Reuben wrote in his best seller *Everything You Ever Wanted to Know About Sex but Were Afraid to Ask*:

As the estrogen is shut off, a woman comes as close as she can to being a man. Increased facial hair, deepened voice, obesity, and the decline of breasts and female genitalia all contribute to a masculine appearance. Coarsened features, enlargement of the clitoris, and gradual baldness complete the tragic picture. Not really a man but no longer a functional woman, these individuals live in the world of intersex.

Abuse from so-called experts is especially unforgivable because of the authority they carry. Reuben's statement has rightfully gained notoriety for its bias and inaccuracy. Nevertheless, I include it here because it reveals the neutering myth in its most blatant form. This is the myth that strikes terror into the heart of women: the myth that becoming neutered is physically inevitable—no matter that these denizens of "the world of intersex" sound unlike the real women you and I know.

Because of this insidious myth, women often wonder if they will lose their sex desire as they age. As a forty-nine-year-old English journalist said to me, "I am in a real panic to remain sexually interested. I would do whatever necessary to keep sexually interesting and interested—but I don't know how it works and I have no confidence that one can keep on."

We need to combat the myth of physiological neutering before we can tackle the psychological neutering that is based upon it. For it is not true that at menopause estrogen production is "shut off." Estrogen production, no longer needed at the higher levels necessary for fertility, does decline markedly, but some estrogen is produced (by the ovaries and the adrenals) throughout life.

When women are no longer flooded with estrogen, their hormonal balance shifts and the secondary sexual characteristics that were the hallmarks of fertility may become less prominent. However, women still remain women, physically, sexually, and emotionally. Indeed, what else would they be?

Are women defined only as babymaking machines in active service? If so, a woman *is* "less a woman" after youth. If not, an older woman is no less a woman, but just a different woman. Why should we accept the illogical idea that a woman is only a woman for thirty years of her life, and then, like Cinderella's sisters, squeeze ourselves into this absurdly small slipper?

The end of the period of fertility is only that. It in no way reduces women's sexual and feminine feelings and capabilities—it may, in fact, increase them. The androgenic hormones and *not* estrogen are responsible for desire (libido), and as estrogen declines it competes less with these androgens. (Shere Hite reports that many women hit the peak of their sexual desire around menstruation—precisely the time when estrogen is lowest.) Thus, hormonally speaking, there is every reason to feel sexier after menopause.

Of course, age brings changes. Both men and women experience moderate amounts of wear and tear on the sexual apparatus—as well as on the knees, eyes and so forth. Due to lower levels of sex hormone production, both men and women may experience changes in weight and sleep patterns, reduced hair growth, loss of hair color, and loss of genital tissue.

Women's vaginal mucosa thins and takes longer to lubricate, particularly when regular sex has not been available. (This is the most usual reason for declining sexual activity in women.) In men, the reduction of testosterone production, of penile erectile capacity, and of sperm count are well documented.

The myth that older women are neuter can be used to explain away the declining sexual interest of their male peers. Masters and Johnson tell us that it is our responsibility to keep interested in *them*, and that if they lose interest in *us*, it is, again, our fault. This is scapegoating in scientific dress:

> The female partner that incites boredom may have lost herself in the demands of her children, in social activities, in an

individual career, or in any combination of interests extrinsic to the marital focus. By their own admission, many of the women interviewed no longer showed sexual interest in, or sexual concern for, their husbands . . . the ego of the aging male is especially vulnerable to rejection, either real or illusional.

Female egos, on the other hand, can presumably take endless punishment, even at the hands of sex researchers (or perhaps our egos are assumed to decline with our estrogen levels).

Betty, Xanthippe, and Blanche

There are basically three variants on the myth of the neutered woman. One is Betty Crocker, the modern madonna, who smiles eternally from the shelf. Betty is sometimes known as "grandma." Hers is the path of least resistance and most security. This path goes nowhere. It only leads back inside the house, into the holy of holies of the temple of domesticity—the kitchen. Betty also lives a lot inside her own head; outward expansion is beyond her. Betty is well loved, the image of contentment—but why does her smile seem as baked-on as her perfect pie crust? An inordinate number of older women are valued as Betty Crocker. But some, like the late Malvina Reynolds, resist being packaged this way: "I have to fight a popular image of me that is totally distorted and that I do not like at all: the 'Singing Grandmother,' the rocking chair personality. That is not me."

The second variant is that of the harridan, the modern Xanthippe, the shrew nobody wants to bother to tame. She competes successfully with men and thereby relinquishes all hope of love. She is alternately respected and belittled—but always resented. She probably works because she is "frustrated," but her erotic desires (if they do exist) are funny or disgusting. Powerful women in public life risk getting saddled with this image, and our repository of mother-in-law jokes (too well known to need repeating here) is based on this Xanthippe archetype.

In their study of women in Israeli kibbutzim, Lionel Tiger and

Joseph Shepher found that older, powerful men usually had their pick of women, but that older women leaders had sex lives conspicuous by their absence. For women, the trade-off is power for sexuality; evidently both chocolate and vanilla are only for men.

The third variant is a non-image, really—that of the sad shade, the has-been, the invisible nobody who often tries to cling to a faded youth: Blanche DuBois without the Southern charm. She is a victim, and the subject of pitiless jokes, such as this story by Herb Caen in the *San Francisco Chronicle*:

> I must say we have some odd stories today. Even odder than usual. Even. Odd. Care to hear about a 72-yr.-old woman who likes to vacuum in the nude? Thought not. She lives in Union City, on the Alvarado–Niles road, with a bus stop right in front of her house. Last wk. she complained to the Union City transit dept. that peeping toms and even janes were looking into her window from the buses, which sounds a little ridiculous. A 72-yr.-old woman with a great body? Spozzible, I spoze. She won her point, however. The bus stop, used by Union City and AC transit, is being moved 100 yards down the block. If she is so concerned about people gazing upon her old bod, why doesn't she pull the shades or close the curtains? "Sometimes I forget," she says coyly. I'd give you her name but who cares.

Older women are usually seen as either Betty, Xanthippe, or Blanche—alone or in various combinations. But lurking behind these stereotypes is the attitude of disgust and loathing at the idea of mature female desire.

Sexual Self-Actualization

Women are neutered precisely at the time when their sexuality is potentially at its height, and when they are freest to exercise it. Sally Binford, a sex researcher, has written, "The older woman is an emotionally seasoned veteran who has, just through the process of living, learned an enormous amount about relationships and their emotional and sexual components. Having this depth of field against which to measure new experience is an exceedingly valuable asset. By the time a woman reaches middle age, her own sexuality is familiar to her, and age in no way diminishes her capacity for enjoyment. In many ways it enhances it; not only does she know more than she did at twenty or thirty, but her orgasmic capacity has probably increased, and she is apt to be a more skilled and sensitive partner than she was when she was younger and less experienced."

Many women without an opportunity to put their feelings to the test intuit that they have a greater capacity for lovemaking than ever before; the greater self-knowledge of the middle years also extends to a knowledge of one's passionate nature: "I know I am or would be a better lover than ever because I am a more loving person now than ever," an Italian woman told me. "I finally can forget about *myself.*"

And a recent study conducted by Dr. Nan Corby of the University of Southern California is revealing. In a sample of about 1,700 women over fifty, 70 percent experienced a moderate to strong interest in sex. When the test population was broken down into smaller age groups, it turned out that a moderate to strong interest in sex was reported by over half the women in each age group up to eighty, and by 32 percent of women eighty and over. Other American researchers like Hite, Rubin, and Thorsen have obtained similar findings. In France, Jeanne Cressanges sent a questionnaire to 575 women over forty, and two-thirds said they were more sexually *awakened* now than at twenty or thirty.

The mature years, after children are grown, are also, at least theoretically, prime time for sexual liberation, although the economic dependency of many older women can interfere. But at least there is no need to keep up appearances for children, or to stay with a partner who is unsatisfying in order to keep the nest in order.

Sexual experience enriches the body. Cumulative excitation develops a dense network of nerves and blood vessels in the tissues surrounding the vagina, thus leading to increased physiological capacity for sexual response. Psychologically too, sexual responsiveness never need stop growing or refining. Like our other human capacities, it can move from a purely physical act to one that is a total spiritual communion. Older lovers speak of the quality of their lovemaking, the fruit of all their accumulated living. Self-actualization, as psychologist Abraham Maslow tells us, is sexual as well as psychological.

Because of the neutering myth, we have few descriptions of the maturing of female sexuality. But, ever the exception, Isadora Duncan in her autobiography describes her sexual self-actualization:

> How I pity those poor women whose pallid, narrow creed precludes them from the magnificent and generous gift of the Autumn of Love. Such was my poor mother, and to this absurd prejudice she owed the aging and illness of her body at the epoch when it should have been most splendid, and the partial collapse of a brain that had been magnificent. I was once the timid prey, then the aggressive Bacchante, but now I close over my lover as the sea over the bold swimmer, enclosing, swirling, encircling him in waves of cloud and fire.

Neutering and Patriarchy

Duncan's vision of mature female sexuality is dangerous to our patriarchal social organization. Men fear the power of women in a way that women know is fantastical. They blow us up to be larger than life, and then expend a great deal of energy to cut us down to size. The roots of this male fear of the power of women, says Dorothy Dinnerstein, are in our long mother-dominated infancy.

It is really mother who is larger than life; her power is truly overwhelming to the infant. When she responds to its cries, her body is the source of all pleasure, comfort—of life itself—and when she denies the child, she is also the great void, the cause of all misery and deprivation. But baby girls grow up to become women and mothers themselves. They learn firsthand that they are not archetypes but human beings. Men, however, never learn to demystify women.

They take control of us to control what they think is the capricious and devastating power that resides in our bodies. Sexual repression of women is the outcome. In the traditional world of patriarchy, sexuality itself is suspect. Libido is thought to come in female guise, trapping the unsuspecting male. As the *Malleus Maleficarum*, a classic treatise on witchcraft, says: "All witchcraft comes from carnal lust, which in women is insatiable . . . wherefore for the sake of fulfilling their lusts they consort with devils. . . . It is sufficiently clear that it is no matter for wonder that there are more women than men found infected with the heresy of witchcraft."

Older women are particularly dangerous. Often widowed or single, they are no longer under control of father or husband. Alone and sexually savvy, they are "free-floating radicals," potential threats to the system. No wonder their sexuality is put down as either disgusting, ridiculous, or nonexistent.

The nuclear family is the nest where this putdown is hatched.

The family is the sole arena where women have power. For this reason, their relationship with their children tends to be very close and controlling. This intensity of the nuclear family romance leads to hangups on mother. Teenage sons tend to resolve the conflict by seeing mother as sexless. Teenage daughters, too, have their own rivalrous reasons for neutering mom. According to researchers, they almost universally have trouble seeing their mothers as sexual beings. And mom collaborates in her own neutering by putting her parenting role ahead of her role as a woman. She placates her daughter and releases her son by playing Betty Crocker.

We can see this entire drama in exaggerated form in traditional patriarchal societies like Spain, Italy, Greece and so many others. Women in these cultures are always under a man's thumb. The young girl is controlled through the virginity norm by her father and brothers. Later, after marriage, she is controlled through the fidelity norm by her husband, and becomes a full-fledged matron.

Single older women—usually widows—are encased in punitive, nunlike black garments that neuter them. Off to church they go, entrusted to the care of another man—He on the cross—the only one who can receive the intensity of their feelings without fear. There is no greater testimony to the sexuality of older women than the rigor with which it is controlled in these societies.

When we look at other cultures and other eras, we can see that there is nothing natural about neutering. In Polynesia, for example, older women called "tutus" (for "grandmother" or "great-aunt") used to instruct the young in sexual technique. Zaftig and sexy, even today they dance voluptuously, joke loudly at weddings, and preside at church bazaars where they entertain with explicit sexual license. It is no accident that Polynesian cultures are not patriarchal. They give women—and sex—a much higher status than do our Western cultures. And not surprisingly, they also give women an honored place.

In France, older women traditionally played the role of sexual initiator. Among the aristocracy everyone had white (powdered) hair and age was no barrier to sexual activity. Today in the black community, older women suffer every conceivable oppression *except* loss of sexuality. And in the few societies where human beings are known to live past 100, as in Vilcabamba in Peru and Hunza and Abkhasia in Russia, sexual activity for both men and women persists throughout life.

Sexuality and Personhood

But neutering is more than sexual deprivation. It is the taking away of our sense of human identity. By telling us that we are not really women anymore, neutering strikes at the deep roots of our sense of self that are linked to gender.

Gender is what society makes of the biological fact of sex difference. It is the most basic of all social roles. The moment we are born, we are wrapped in a pink or blue blanket; gender is already placed on us. In fact, we do not have a self apart from being gendered.

Gender is internalized very early, at about age two or three.

Our sense of existence is linked so intimately with our idea of ourselves as male or female that without this we lose our fundamental psychic bearings and fall into the abyss of being no one at all. The Nazis knew this when, to break women's spirits, they shaved their heads and dressed them in sacks. And Carlfred Broderick, a sex researcher, writes: "I have seen women of 70 and older in deep depression, almost a catatonic depression that nobody could seem to get them out of, until somebody thought of taking them to a beauty parlor. This experience was somehow reassertive of themselves as people of value, somebody worth responding to."

Neutering also denies life energy, otherwise known as libido, elan vital, eros. This primal stream which pulses through all creation takes endless forms. In the human creature it divides in two, flowing into the channels we call male and female. Thus the life force is sexually expressed and diverted into two different destinies. Each of our styles of being-in-the-world tells what we have made of this original current which was our birthright.

The connection of sexual energy with life energy has a physiological basis. The same hormones that stimulate libido affect other physiological processes: protein synthesis, salt and water balance, bone growth and resorption, cardiovascular function, and possibly the immune system. Thus, throughout life, sexuality is connected with well-being, vitality, and longevity.

Ani Mander describes a personal experience in this connection: "Arthritic pain in me has a lot to do with diet, but also with sex. Orgasm releases endorphins in the body—they take care of pain. I have actually felt this happen in the middle of sex."

Freud devoted his professional life to the explication of this relationship between life energy and sexuality. He defined libido as the biologically given drive toward pleasure. According to him, an infant sucking at the breast was engaged in (oral) sexual behavior, much as two adults making love were engaged in (genital) sexual behavior. He thought all elaborations of personality and culture were deflections of this primal current.

Our gender is its first form of expression. We participate in the dance of life not as neutral entities but as men or women. The three basic elements in the dance are our elan vital, our biological sexuality, and our (feminine or masculine) gender. These elements are in constant interplay and cannot be separated. The full activation of all of them gives us an unparalleled feeling of wholeness—as in love. And our connectedness to any of the three elements tends to generalize to the others. A friend told me about an especially life-filled seminar she attended in which Margaret Mead was one of the participants. "The dialogue was really exciting," she said, "and as I heard those people listen and pick up on each others' ideas I felt an almost sexual pleasure from their interchange." It is in this sense that we can say with Freud that everything is sexual.

Sexuality pervades all of our meaningful relationships. It is there between friends, parents and children, teachers and students, a good salesman and his customer. And we all know the moribund feeling of human exchanges when this "stuff of life" is absent.

Our use of language reveals that we know sexuality is generalized beyond the genitals. *Mate* means a biological sex partner, but also (in British English) a close friend—someone with whom we share a bond of intimacy. An *attractive* person is someone we feel like getting to *know*—in the biblical sense or not. The word *lovemaking* itself means more than genital contact. We are *turned on* or *seduced* by ideas as well as bodies, and when we get *screwed* or *fucked over* we feel we have been used, i.e., that our personhood has not been respected. ("Is the screw you're getting worth the screw you're getting?" I was once asked.)

Neutering, therefore, is not just sexual rejection; it could not possibly be. It is a threat to our basic foothold in the world: our self. Thus neutering threatens our energetic being-in-the-world—our ability to desire strongly, to become ecstatic, to hold on, to play, to dance, to synthesize, to embrace, to take, to give, to surrender, to merge into oneness, and to create. Whether or not we have a sexual partner is almost irrelevant to the neutering we experience apart from our private lives. Older women as a class are all affected by this prevailing climate to some extent—even those of us who because of exceptional looks, talent, or power think we are immune.

Some women actually felt neutering happening to them as a kind of deadening. They talked about an absence of aliveness and of sexual desire that was not a natural falling away. Something was gone, or, more accurately, missing. This feeling of a missing part is the clue that life energy is being suppressed.

> I have not been out at night because I have lost the art of conversation after twenty-eight years of caring for children and staying home watching TV. Am I lazy, a moron, why am I content with such a narrow existence? It is peaceful, but . . . *is this all?*

> My problem is complete lack of interest in sex. I do not feel frustrated, deprived, or neurotic, but know that I should be. Heavens, I used to be a normal, sexy woman—will I ever feel sexy again?

When women talk about their fear of becoming neutered, the concern they have about turning off would not be there if sex was just an itch that no longer needed to be scratched. What they are afraid of is the disconnection from their gender and from their vital energy. A publisher says:

> I would be very unhappy to lose my sexual attractiveness— my husband says that's nonsense, you can go on forever—but I'm not talking just about fucking. Even as a publisher talking to a man, there's sex involved. I would miss it if that tension were not there.

Acknowledging the connection between sexuality and life energy does not mean that we are obligated to be sexually active. Sister Marie, a fifty-four-year-old nun, spoke to me about the subtle diverting of sexuality into other channels:

> Celibacy is another way of releasing physical energy, as opposed to a long-standing physical relationship. Your primary love energy is moving along with the Lord. It is not a denial

of sexual energy—I am sure the saints were filled with physical energy and experienced themselves sexually.

We were taught to deny the reality of the body: we were
told that allowing any pleasure would lead to sexual pleasure
and we'd be in big trouble. But because we denied the reality
of our bodies we never took them to prayer with us and it affected prayer adversely. This has changed today. Now we talk
about sex among ourselves . . . what does it mean for religious
life? Celibacy is a state of mind that goes beyond non-engage-
ment of the genitals. We are more honest now. I remember a
conversation while we were darning socks. A thirty-five-year-
old sister said, "I'll be so glad when I'm forty and I won't
have to bother with these sex drives anymore." A sister of seventy answered in a low voice, "Oh yeah?" She didn't look up,
though; she kept on darning socks!

The key is the acknowledgment of sexuality in all its forms. It is
no accident that nuns are considered *brides* of Christ. They are
not told they have no sexual desires; quite the contrary. Celibacy,
moreover, is a voluntary condition, while the neutered state is
not.

The connection between sex and personhood is compellingly
articulated by Zoe Moss in *Sisterhood Is Powerful:*

Listen to me! Think what it is like to have most of your life
ahead and to be told that you are obsolete! Think what it is
like to feel attraction, desire, affection towards others, and
want to tell them about yourself, to feel that assumption on
which self-respect is based, that you are worth something, and
that if you like someone, surely he will be pleased to know
that. To be, in other words, still a living woman, and to be
told every day that you are not a woman but a tired object
that should disappear. That you are not a person but a joke.
Well, I am a bitter joke. I am bitter and frustrated and
wasted, but don't you pretend for a minute as you look at me,
forty-three, fat, and looking exactly my age, that I am not as
alive as you are and that I do not suffer from the category into
which you are forcing me.

What Neutering Feels Like

First, neutering comes as a shock. Like the child who abruptly has the breast taken away when a younger sibling appears, we too are stunned when suddenly deprived of the milk of recognition.

Other deprived groups have not had to confront the effects of withdrawal. A black is born black and learns quite early that he will have to deal with overt mistreatment throughout his life. This is terrible, but consistent. But what if one were white and then turned black? The shock of neutering is no less disarming.

John Howard Griffin, a white journalist, chose to have this experience in 1959 and wrote about it in his book *Black Like Me*. Griffin used skin-coloring chemicals in order to pass for black in the Deep South. His experience "traces the changes that occur to the heart and body and intelligence when a so-called first class citizen is cast on the junkheap of second class citizenship." Even though Griffin had chosen this role and knew it was temporary, he could not tolerate it for more than a few weeks at a time, and had to reenter the white world periodically to save his sanity. Early in his journey he already knew defeat:

> As I sat in the sunlight, a great heaviness came over me . . . I noted too that my face had lost animation. In repose, it had taken on the strained disconsolate expression that is written on the countenance of so many Southern Negroes. My mind had become the same way, dozing empty for long periods. Like the others in my condition, I was finding life too burdensome. I felt a great hunger for something merely pleasurable, for something people call fun.

Change the words "Southern Negroes" to "older women" to see if the passage still works. How many do you know?

We often say we are shocked to find ourselves aging. "Aging— it's the worst thing that can happen to a woman," I was told by a barmaid. "It comes as such a shock—one day you look in the mirror and there are all those lines and bags and sags." These changes are shocking, in part, because of our denial of aging. But the neutering we experience because of them can only compound the shock.

Mostly, neutering feels like rejection. The pain is expressed with varying degrees of openness:

I had a lover who was considerably younger than me. Our relationship gradually became more and more platonic—now we are just friends. I broke it off. He admitted sometimes he thought I was too old for him. I knew he was seeing younger women. I didn't feel good about it after that.

I was very proud. I never wanted anyone to know what I was going through. I tried to give the impression that I had a very gay life. Sometimes I went away just to give the impression that I was busy. Because I'm ashamed of self-pity, I don't want to cry for myself.

I have aging women friends and we enjoy each other. It's really not an empty existence, but ten years ago it was. I was really sensationally beautiful, and I realized I'd never have a profound lover again after many relationships. This was hard to give up.

I function perfectly well professionally—I just feel an ache and an emptiness all the time that will not go away.

I am inescapably fifty-six, and how can a woman of my age go looking for a lover as a man could? Every day of my life I long for a loving sex relationship and every day I try to come to terms with the heartbreaking fact that for me it is all over.

Different friends of mine are "over the hill," you might say. Nobody wants them anymore—for anything. Gee, when their husbands go they'll really be up a creek. But I'm used to being alone.

Collaborating with Neutering

The neutered condition is a disease we catch from the environment we live in. We could remain healthier if we had more resistance to it. Unfortunately, we do not. Neutering works through our own cooperation. We do it to ourselves.

Why would we do such a thing? Given the fact that many of us retain our desire for living and loving as we age, how is it that we are willing to condone the neutering process to the extent that we do? Why are we willing to treat our sexuality as a private, embarrassing vice? And why do we often participate in turning ourselves off altogether?

The answer comes in two parts. First is the fact that society has insidious ways of wielding persuasive power over us. Second, we have our own reasons for cooperating.

The social pressures on us today tell us we should be content. We are deprived, but we are told that we actually are not missing anything, that the state of deprivation is due to our natures. It is as if we were back in the days when the public said that black people actually liked slavery because they were happy-go-lucky and dependent.

The name of this game is Gaslight: "Everything is fine, and if you don't like it you are crazy." It is a painful game.

When one is overtly vilified, one can at least gather support and mount a defense. But to be treated with amusement or a kind of empty courtesy by the very people who deny our human reality robs us of the clarity to know that a defense is called for. Probably the primary accomplishment of the (younger) women's movement has been to end this pain of not having one's oppression validated. This validation needs to be extended to older women as well.

Meanwhile, we accept our treatment meekly and silently because we are not even sure that anything is really happening. To talk about neutering is in a sense a contradiction in terms; the more successfully one is neutered, the less one is aware that there is anything wrong.

The psychologist Kurt Lewin found that if children were placed behind a glass window filled with appealing but inaccessible toys, they soon behaved as if the toys were not there. We also act as if we are not missing anything.

In San Francisco, a women-over-forty group showed a film about the people in Vilcabamba, Peru, who are reputed to live to be over 100. Four reasons were given for their longevity: good diet, exercise, low stress, and regular sex. In the discussion that followed, the articulate women present commented extensively on the first *three* reasons for longevity—but *nobody* even mentioned sex!

Our silence is also due to sheer embarrassment. A woman must feel very secure to admit publicly that she is being rejected. We feel vulnerable enough as it is without contributing to our "bad press." Face-saving, in fact, may lead us to collaborate with neutering. "Oh well, we don't want it anyway" is our sour-grapes rationalization for accepting the situation.

Society engenders agreement in us through a psychological mechanism that Anna Freud called "identification with the aggressor." We ally ourselves with those who have power over us, in an unconscious attempt to propitiate them. In doing so, we internalize their value system, no matter how destructive it may be to ourselves. One of the most striking instances of the workings of this mechanism was observed by Bruno Bettelheim in the concentration camps. He noticed that some of the inmates actually adopted the attitudes, beliefs, and personal mannerisms of their guards! In the same way, we acquiesce in the double standard of aging, even though it runs counter to both our welfare and our internal perceptions. Over the long years of our upbringing, it becomes deeply embedded in our psyches—but we don't even know it's there.

Our other motivation for collaborating with neutering stems from our family relationships. It can be convenient for other members of our families to see us as asexual, as discussed earlier. It takes the pressure off our husbands, who may be having their own sexual difficulties. It releases our sons to form sexual relationships with women their own age. It reassures our daughters that we are not in competition with them. Insofar as we put our families' needs first, and we often do, we may simply find it easier to knuckle under to the subtle pressures upon us.

And we must also add that in a society as ambivalent as ours is about sex, some women happily call a halt to what was never a very satisfying part of their lives.

In all these ways, neutering makes the double standard our standard—so much a part of ourselves that we don't even notice its inconsistencies. It can even become a source of personal gratification. We pride ourselves on behaving with "dignity" (which usually means not having any fun) and put down other women who refuse to climb onto the shelf.

Thus we become our own worst enemies. Women everywhere adopt the double standard of aging as their own.

> As I get older I worry whether my lover will continue to desire me. I see no difference in him—no aging in the bodies of men, but a lot in mine. Oh yes, of course they get gray hair and wrinkles, but I like that.

> A little weight on a man does no harm, it's to be expected after a certain age, but on a woman—ugh! It spoils her figure and makes her unattractive.

We start to believe we are getting decrepit:

> I find myself thinking, I can't take this dance class, I can't go motorcycling—even my mind is too old to take a really challenging course! I know it's ridiculous—but those voices in my head are there.

And we start to think of ourselves as sexless, prudish, or unattractive:

> I find I get "prissy" now that I'm not "with" anyone. When people talk about staying in bed instead of going to the movies, or if they make off-color jokes, I feel this shot of fear

and then I think, That's disgusting—why do they say these things in front of *me?* But when I was doing those things myself, the same kind of jokes seemed funny to me.

I used to scan the bus for interesting men to talk to—sit next to. Now I don't do it because I don't consider myself an interesting and sexy person—so I don't put out the vibe. So I collaborate with that shit myself.

I have had a strong sex drive all my life. But as I aged that changed. I don't know if I'm less horny now because of the lack of available partners or if it's physiological—but the body is less beautiful and I just would rather not.

We reject or hate who we are:

The best age to be is thirty-two, because at thirty-two you've more or less figured out what life is about—you're neither too young nor too old to catch the eye of anyone from eighteen to eighty. . . . Men really go for women around then, men of any age—you have enough experience to be an intelligent listener instead of a talker. You've probably had a child or two, which gives you a sense of what life is about, but age hasn't taken hold of you yet.

I met an old lover I hadn't seen for fifteen years, since I was thirty. I was a little nervous. Suddenly I noticed him staring at my hand on the table. I looked down and suddenly saw it through his eyes. And it was a forty-five-year-old hand. And you know, I love my hands, they can do a lot! But at that moment I felt a surge of hate for my hands—the wrinkles, the veins, the age spots—and I hated him for making me feel that way and I hated myself too.

Neutering invades our pores. The neutering myth becomes our reality; it creates its own reality. Whenever we "in decency" give up the right to sexual fulfillment, that is neutering. When we meekly accept our treatment as if we deserve it, that is neutering. When we look at ourselves and despise our bodies and faces, that is neutering. When we think that living a half-life is the normal condition for older women, that is neutering.

The Results of Neutering

As older women today, we have a difficult choice to make. Either we submit to the prevailing norms, or we pit our internal feelings against the massive social pressures to neuter us. In the first case, we become what they want us to be. We give up the struggle, and try as much as possible to suppress our potential for greater loving and living. In the second, we are involved in a continual expenditure of energy to maintain our morale and our good feelings about ourselves in the absence of social reinforcement.

Mostly we do both. We vacillate between bending to the pressures and opposing them. As Zoe Moss puts it, the confusion is crazymaking. "To be told when you have half your years still to wade through and when you don't feel inside much different than you did at twenty (you are still you!—you know that), to be told then that you are cut off from expressing yourself sexually and even in friendship, drives many women crazy—often literally so."

Much as in adolescence, one loses track of who one is. But with the difference that the adolescent is motivated to claim her new identity and is rewarded for doing so. The older woman, on the other hand, is penalized. Like the teenager's, her image wavers in the glass—but it is further obscured by the shadows of her own dread.

Perhaps the women whose aging is least painful today are those who feel the least dissonance between themselves and the Betty Crocker image. For women who truly accept this role, midlife poses less of a problem and brings its own rewards. Everything in our lives impels us to accept this solution.

Women are used to making do. *J'ai mis de l'eau dans mon vin* ("I have mixed water in my wine"), as one Frenchwoman put it. How many of us have made our peace with half-life in our middle years, simply because no other options exist? We operate within a frame of reference which makes it difficult for us even to conceive of later life as a time of as much importance, excitement, and validity as our childbearing years.

The result of neutering is that women turn off. We learn to accept a life in a nether world of pastels, out of touch with the energy and full use of ourselves that dimly somewhere we know is there. We learn to downplay what I call our "ex's": our excellence, our exuberance, our expertise, our experimentalism, our experience, our excitement. Mediocrity becomes the acceptable, in fact obligatory, modus vivendi. "No sooner was their youth, with the little force and impetus characteristic of youth, done, than they stopped growing," says Katherine Mansfield in her journal. "At the very moment that one felt that now was the time to gather oneself together, to use one's whole strength, to take control, to be an adult; in fact, they seemed content to swap the darling wish of their hearts for innumerable little wishes."

Talking about neutering will not make it go away. But the first step in curing any disease is to name it and to understand how it works. This alone can strengthen our resistance to it.

6

MIXED MESSAGES: OLDER WOMEN AND THE MEDIA

They call them age spots.
I call them ugly!
But what's a woman to do?
        Porcelana TV commercial

BARBARA WALTERS

SANDRA O'CONNOR

JULIA CHILD

BILLIE JEAN KING

ELIZABETH TAYLOR

MILLICENT FENWICK

KATHARINE GRAHAM

YOKO ONO

BETTY FRIEDAN

MARTHA GRAHAM

JANE FONDA

BETTY FORD

JEANE KIRKPATRICK

JOYCE BROTHERS

HELEN GURLEY BROWN

ANN LANDERS

ABBY VAN BUREN

SUSAN BROWNMILLER

JACQUELINE ONASSIS

PHYLLIS SCHLAFLY

BELLA ABZUG

NANCY REAGAN

GLORIA STEINEM

KATHARINE HEPBURN

LILLIAN HELLMAN

LUCILLE BALL

This is my list of highly visible older American women. It is a short one and in many ways a strange one—wealth, position, genuine achievement, and noisy notoriety all mixed together. Your list may be somewhat different, but I know it could not be much longer, particularly as regards women of exceptional accomplishment. For every Barbara Walters there are ten Dan Rathers. There are only two female senators (Paula Hawkins and Nancy Landon Kassebaum) out of a hundred. There is one female publisher of a major newspaper, Katharine Graham. In fact, only 0.8 percent of full-time working women make $25,000 or more, compared with 12 percent of men.

We hear very little about older women in the media. When we are mentioned at all, usually someone from the above list is reliably trotted out. And the list hasn't changed much, either, over the last decade. Ultimately, it is a list of token women. It gives an erroneous impression of great strides for older women, but we see few honest portrayals of either our real achievements or of our problems. What we do see is a distortion which leaves us ultimately confused.

Impact of the Media

The impact of the media is hard to overestimate. If we combine time spent listening, reading, and viewing over a lifetime, the sum total is greater than any other activity in which we engage, except sleep. The average American dedicates four hours a day to the electronic media (TV and radio).

The quintessential mass medium is television, in both its standardization of message and in its magical power over us. An amazing 99 percent of us own a TV, and in the average home sets are on for more than six hours daily. Women over fifty-five spend more time watching TV than any other group—about five hours a day. More women than men attribute the enjoyment of their day to TV, and the audiences for daytime soaps are 71 percent female.

Television images have a special power to bypass our critical faculties. There is no picture on a TV screen. All that actually exists is a constantly shifting configuration of pinpoints of light moving at electronic speeds—too fast for us to perceive them. These dots impinge upon our retinas and are processed by our brains into images inside our heads. We have no chance to decide whether we wish to assimilate these images, the way we do, say, when we look at a photograph. The process of seeing and absorbing the image are one and the same. For this reason advertisers are not unduly worried about negative responses to their commercials. They know that even disgust with an ad barely threatens this unconscious level of acceptance.

TV images have a "realer than real" quality. The world portrayed on TV is not the real world (which includes large numbers of children, poor, old, unattractive, racially different, and just downright unclassifiable people who do undramatic things). It is instead a crisis-filled, theatrical, and prettied-up world which seems to be run largely by doctors and policemen. But this world comes across with a marvelous intensity, as a kind of exemplar which makes the real world seem like a pale shadow flickering on the walls of Plato's cave.

The familiar screen is in fact the modern magic mirror. Its picture of us is the picture we believe. Even fiction is somehow perceived as "true." Marcus Welby received 250,000 requests for medical advice during his first five years of TV "practice"! And ironically, the truth begins to have the same "canned" quality as the fiction. ("What is that movie you are watching?" someone asked. "That's not a movie, that's El Salvador" was the response.) Life is entertainment; entertainment is life.

TV programs, because they are served up to unbelievable numbers of people at once, cater to the lowest common denominator. Thirty million typically are watching the same evening show, and up to one hundred million could be! Subtlety or innovation is unlikely. With a moving image and a brief time frame, meaning must be conveyed as quickly as possible. This leads to reliance on stereotypical characters and plots. The conventional image becomes a kind of shorthand understood by everyone—oh yes, there is the tough but compassionate reporter (cop, doctor); there is the brave but ultimately dependent blonde (brunette, redhead). These images exist only to move the plot forward, yet my daughters discuss the motivations of the cast of "General Hospital" with more involvement than the motivations of their friends.

Important social issues that cannot be covered in TV shorthand get short shrift. The subtleties of the women's liberation movement, for example, are harder to convey than conflicts between pro- and anti-abortionists, so we get more of the latter and less of the former. If you want to be on TV, you stand a better chance if you oversimplify and polarize.

And, needless to say, the TV world, like the media world in general, is heavily controlled by young, male people.

Studies show that people are affected by what they see on TV. The *New England Journal of Medicine* reports that heavy viewers were more likely to have poor health habits and unrealistic beliefs in the magic of medicine. Heavy viewers also consistently overestimated the proportion of health professionals, athletes, entertainers, and law enforcement personnel in the population, while light viewers made more accurate judgments, based on real-life experience.

Media Messages: Symbolic Annihilation

Any discussion about older women in the media must be seen against the background of the sexist hiring, programming, and advertising that are still the rule.

Women are usually shown as passive homebodies, dependent on men, younger than men, victims or sex objects, and above all, consumers. And according to a recent issue of *Newsweek*, television portrays less than 20 percent of married women with children working outside the home—as compared with more than 50 percent in real life. This article also reports that portrayals of older women "transmit negative impressions. In general, they are cast as silly, stubborn, sexually inactive and eccentric." And, most important, we are underrepresented.

Researcher Gaye Tuchman describes the overall treatment of women in the media as "symbolic annihilation." On TV commercials, for example, there are three all-male ads to each all-female ad. Our panty liners and douches come to us with female voice-overs, but in general voice-overs are 87 percent male. Apart from soap operas (where male actors are still a majority), there are two men for every woman on television. "T & A" programming, as it is called, is ubiquitous, often replacing violent shows when public protest forces them off the air.

What is true about the symbolic annihilation of women is exponentially true for older women. We are just not there. We can all think of exceptions. But the rule is that we are not in or on the magazines. Not on television or radio. Not in the newspapers. This is especially true for poor and minority women.

Although more than 59 percent of women are over forty, TV commercials show only 25 percent of women over forty, while showing 45 percent of men over forty. Women are also younger than men in dramas and soap operas and on quiz shows, and female villains averaged forty-two to forty-seven years old while female heroes averaged twenty-nine.

Melanie, a longtime actress of the legitimate stage, gave me another look at symbolic annihilation. She is contemplating a face lift. "I want to do television work," she said, "because that's where the money is. But people don't like to look at wrinkles on TV. As far as TV is concerned, wrinkles don't exist. Even grandmothers have no wrinkles on TV. I don't like it, but it happens to be the standard. I was devastated by reviews last season commenting on my wrinkles. I decided then and there on the operation."

Susan Arnell is a forty-year-old television commercial actress with a well-scrubbed, American look. She started her career in her early twenties and has learned firsthand how to change her image in order to keep working:

At first, they always had me running on the beach, drinking a Tab or Coke. From twenty-eight to thirty, I was always a stewardess. Don't ask me why—I didn't *ever* want to be a stewardess. Today I would never be cast as one, even though we know that there are older women on planes. In my thirties, I was the young mother with toddlers, advertising lots of foods—bread, lunch meats, the sort of thing kids eat. I have a special wardrobe consisting of denim wrap-around skirts, Levi's shirts with a sweater tied around, shirtwaist dresses.

Whenever they say "Midwest housewife" I know exactly what that means. You have to know how to dress for the part when you go for an interview, because they don't know what they want until you give them the image. Now I am the young executive, the beige suit, medium heels, neat and orderly—that sort of thing. Or else I do the supermarket ads, projecting the image of the "smart shopper"—using a lot of "strong" words like "basic," "economy," "value." I've said loads of those things you never hear real people saying—like "Gee, Marilyn, how did you get your shirt so white?" or "I always shop at ——————— Market because the produce is so fresh and I get such good value for my money."

Susan is starting to experience symbolic annihilation. "One day your age range changes," she said.

———

It can just happen overnight. It's sort of depressing. No one ever told me that twenty-five or thirty-two would be my big earning years. You find it out when you don't get the work. My career is real slow right now. The last few months, I don't even check in. I've lost that feeling of knowing I'll get a job. And I can't psych myself up for it, so I know I won't get it. Lately I've been rejected a lot and I really don't know why. I think I'm starting to be in an age range that no one is focusing on that much.

There is a missing age on television—forty-five to sixty. If you see a business executive, for example, she'll be a forty-five-year-old business executive, not a fifty-five-year-old business executive. Then at sixty there's a small group of women who are white-haired, healthy-looking, grandmotherly types who do the denture creams and so forth.

Symbolic annihilation today comes in modern dress. Daytime TV mothers no longer wear aprons in all their scenes, as they did thirty years ago, and they can say the word "pregnant." In fact, plots unfold against a timely background of drug rings, surrogate motherhood, homosexuality, and so forth. But who are the characters, and what is happening to them? Pick up a copy of *Daytime Digest* if you want to catch up quickly. "Luke Rapes Laura, They Fall in Love." "Maggie Vows to Give Away Her Child." "Lisa Chases After Brad." "Sofia Spies on Carol and Steve."

The media convince us that, like the other folks who are symbolically annihilated—the dark-skinned, the handicapped, the less than beautiful, the foreign, the poor—there is something wrong with us. Otherwise, we would be on television, wouldn't we? And the presence of those older women who pass—or those few exceptions who are always successful and impeccably dressed—serve to convince us that we are hopelessly *wrong*—that we do not even deserve to exist.

We are still portrayed unsympathetically or milked for laughs, like the "dingbat" aunt played by Dodie Goodman on "Diff'rent Strokes" or Jean Stapleton's Edith Bunker. Our sexuality is dubious, if it exists at all. If and when we do have deep emotions, they are usually of the "woman scorned" variety, like Joan Collins' "Alexis" of "Dynasty." Or else we are bitches and witches, dominating family dynasties, like Jane Wyman on "Falcon Crest."

We live vicariously, offering advice and comfort to younger characters whose lives are where the action is. We worry about them, but usually nothing much happens in our own lives, like Jessie Brewer on "General Hospital."

Symbolic annihilation is a numbers game. Quantitative analysis reveals again and again the extent to which older women are conspicuously absent from the media. We may be consciously impressed with the good news (shows like "Alice," "Maude," or "One Day at a Time"), but in the long run this day-in, day-out unarticulated message of invisibility is the one with the deepest impact.

Media Messages: Youth Marketing

It is, of course, in advertising that the hard sell of youth is most blatant, playing on our fears of loneliness and rejection, reinforcing the idea that products are necessary to make us look right. Estée Lauder's age controlling cream. Porcelana, for those ugly age spots. Clairol, to wash that gray right outta your hair, if you want to look younger, *feel* younger, and keep your man fooled. The goal of all advertising, as writer Jerry Mander says, is discontent.

When was the last time you and your husband met for lunch? Is summer sunlight making you look older? Does your skin have the energy to resist wrinkles? Remember how you looked on your wedding day? Do you look younger with your clothes on? Look younger. Look younger. Look younger.

Young people buy more. Most advertising campaigns target people only up to age forty-nine, since older people are seen as more cautious consumers by the advertising industry, with less money to throw around. But older people are now too numerous to neglect as a market, particularly as the post–World War II baby-boom generation begins to move into middle age. Now *we* must expect the hard sell: to be made to want more, to be less satisfied with who we are.

We are likely to be increasingly pressured to look younger than we are—or, as advertising tactfully puts it, "not to let premature signs of age make us look older than we really are." (In adland, all signs of aging are premature.) And we should also expect a continued escalation of the marketing of new technology to push back the clock—from exercise equipment to new surgical and parasurgical techniques.

But the overt marketing of youth, although a business in the billions, is still peanuts compared to the covert selling of youth that the media inflict upon us. Every time a young woman promotes a certain brand of cars, toothpaste, tires, or computers as desirable, she is also by implication selling her image as the desirable kind of woman to be. Repeated hundreds of thousands of times everywhere, this message hits home. It is difficult to conceive of life without the constant bombardment of an image so narrow in its range that most women, young or old, feel obliterated by comparison.

This image is carefully crafted. The following attributes for male and female ideals were recently published in a book on advertising. The feminine ideal:

AGE: 16–30 years.
SKIN COLOR: white. The skin must be smooth and even. Wrinkles, lines, pimples, etc., are not tolerated. She must not have freckles, but a tan is tolerated.
FIGURE: thin to slender.
FACIAL FEATURES: oval, not round, square, or heart-shaped. Quite thin face, definite or suggested "hollow cheeks." High to medium forehead. Medium or small straight nose. Normal ears, neither large nor protruding. Medium to large eyes without any tendency to squint; no glasses. Medium chin, neither square, double, small nor receding. White, even teeth.
HAIR: thick and glossy. Neither gray, thin, nor greasy.

Compare the above with the masculine ideal:

AGE: 16–45 years.
SKIN COLOR: white, preferably tanned. No special demands about smoothness, etc., but pimples are not tolerated.
FIGURE: thin to athletic, neither pot-bellied nor round-shouldered.
FACIAL FEATURES: square to oval face. Can be wider than that of the beautiful woman. High to medium-high forehead. Marked features, firm jaws and strong mouth for example. Powerful to medium large chin, neither double nor fleshy. Eyes of normal size without any tendency to squint and glasses may be worn. Normal (not protruding) ears. Clean shaven, moustache or a beard provided that it is neither long, tangled, nor sparse.
HAIR: either thick tousled, or rather short cut, but not thin, greasy, or sleek. No bald patches. Any color, even gray.

The irony of this situation is that women are generally the purchasing agents for the family, yet there is no corresponding pitch to "sell" merchandise by means of the male physique, apart from occasional cigarette ads. If this double standard works to sell products, as it must, it can only do so if women identify with this female ideal and subconsciously buy it along with the merchandise.

And the women who are most avidly absorbing this message of self-hate are the older, poorer, and probably less-educated for whom television is *the* source of recreation. They seldom see themselves reflected, and they can ill afford to buy the products which they are being manipulated to want.

Media Messages: The Reinforcement of Stereotypes

Within the small number of older women that appear as images, the old stereotypes prevail. We are provincial homebodies, advertising food and cleaning products to give them an aura of integrity. "New, Improved" is old hat. But "natural" and "old-fashioned goodness" are "in." Mrs. Olsen tells us that Folger's tastes like the real stuff, and her age lends the pitch credibility. Particularly as the influence of the women's movement fosters more Charlies and Virginia Slims, the field of dowdy old Betty Crocker is left to the older woman. We have taken over the role of Step'n Fetchit, often appearing fearful and out of control.

Or else we are in need of medical attention: looking distressed because of hemorrhoids or headaches, falling apart because we need estrogen or tranquilizers. "When she can't manage, you can," says the copy on a double-page ad in *U.S. Medicine*, featuring the unhappy life-size face of an older woman who will presumably have her problems solved by Premarin.

Apart from soap and floor wax, we are usually involved with products specific to the older market, like dentures. One would think that an older woman never drank a soft drink, ate a hamburger, or drove an automobile.

Newspapers, too, depend on huge circulations, and lean toward material "in the general interest." They also shape this interest according to their criteria for news. Newspaper people are largely male and what they call news tends to be men talking to men about the things that concern them. Omitted from the news pages is a story about Minnie, an older black woman who behind the scenes is making the Head Start program work in her neighborhood. Omitted is Beatrice, a fifty-four-year-old woman who visits shut-ins and gives them a reason to keep on living. Omitted is the whole world of intimate experience and the processes of life and death involving diapers and sacrifices and personal courage. Although these are serious topics of life as women see them, they are supplanted in favor of the bloodless, remote-from-life decisions that make up most of male talk at business lunches, meetings, and press conferences. A Martian reading the paper would conclude that the world was indeed a man's world, with a few women here and there—most of whom spend a few days a month getting married, and then disappear. I found it easy to cut out every story on older women—compare this with the enormous task of cutting out every story on older men!

Men are not supposed to need information about feelings—particularly women's feelings. So news of the women's movement, though potentially of great significance in the lives of men, is underrepresented. Occasionally, an especially well respected reporter with clout like the New York Times' Judy Klemesrud (who covered the White House Mini-Conference on Aging) can get material on older women into the body of the paper, but generally it is segregated—separate and unequal—on the women's pages. This section becomes a news ghetto, with the rest of the paper being the men's pages.

National magazines operate somewhat differently from media pitched to a general audience. Their circulations are also enormous, in the millions, but their readerships are segmented. There are men's and women's magazines, to begin with. Then there are magazines for women of different ages and income levels, magazines for working women, homemakers' magazines like Family Circle, and crafts magazines.

It is easy to spot magazines oriented toward older women. Instead of a young woman on the cover they usually have cake or a chicken. Medical magazines, on the other hand, feature us as laboratory animals—appearing with great frequency in various stages of obesity, menopausal crisis, or emotional distress.

Because magazines speak directly to women's interests, they are sensitive barometers of current trends. Their messages range from the most blatantly agist advertisements to occasional positive presentations about older women—sometimes occurring simultaneously in the pages of the same magazine, as in *Ms.*

Books and film are less stereotyped than magazines and television; they lend themselves to deeper treatment of older women's issues. The image of women in fiction, nonfiction, medical books, textbooks, children's books, and comic books has been analyzed, but age is seldom mentioned in these studies. Researcher Don Smith, however, did an unusual study. He analyzed "adults only" paperbacks available on newsstands, and found that 64 percent of the women and 46 percent of the men were under thirty, and that the men were not physically described, except for their genitals, while the women were described "down to the last dimple."

Symbolic annihilation is so prevalent that we don't even notice it. Clothing ads in print, for instance, seldom or never feature older women, as this February 1982 article from *OWL*, the Older Women's League newsletter, illustrates:

Media Watch—Catalog Version
June Garrison, OWL member from Washington, like millions of other older women, shops at Sears, but only recently realized their catalog failed to show models with whom she could identify—plenty of men as old as her husband but none of older women. She wrote a letter which eventually reached the national advertising manager. His reply is interesting but not reassuring. "We are very conscious of the importance of our 'older' customers—both women and men, as well as many minorities. And I can assure you that we did include women (and men) much over thirty-five in the above catalog. Furthermore we plan to continue this approach."

If you think, as we do, that he missed the point, check out the nearest Sears catalog, count the women "over thirty-five"

(!) and send your complaint to R. L. Ramseyer, Dept. 744, Sears Tower, Chicago, Ill. 60684.

Even media sources that should know better annihilate us— like many books inspired by the women's movement. Emblematic is Marilyn French's *The Women's Room*, which ends with the heroine, Mira, fortyish, wandering in limbo by the ocean, unable to visualize life after youth. And I ruffled through Gail Sheehy's *Passages* several times thinking I had missed the pages on the female midlife passage that corresponded to the substantial section on men. I hadn't; it wasn't there.

It was especially dismaying to find the supposedly feminist studies of women in the media infected by symbolic annihilation. Research for this chapter was maddeningly difficult because age was seldom indexed separately in studies of sexism. In fact, there were fewer references to older women in these studies than appear in the media themselves!

Symbolic annihilation of older women has not always been the norm. In 1963 Martin U. Martel compared fiction portrayals of older women in magazines from 1890 to 1955. He assumed that these portrayals would reflect the images of older women current in the culture. Martel's study documents the descent into annihilation that took place over the course of this period.

Although their roles were circumscribed, at least in 1890 older women were prominent in women's magazine stories. They were often involved in auntly relationships and close friendships with younger women. By the later period, 1955, such friendships hardly ever appear. Changes in the marital relationship are also striking. In the 1890s, virtue, character, emotional strength, and skill at household management over the course of a lifelong relationship were valued over the "romance" of the early honeymoon period. By 1955, the emphasis has shifted to the early marital years, and marriage value deteriorates after age forty, a loss far greater for the woman than for the man. Martel calls this the "deflation of wifehood." The prime of life has reversed drastically for women from mature middle (in 1890) to young adulthood (in 1955), with the wife gradually losing her authority as the "in-plant manager of the household." Life after forty tends to be seen as anticlimactic, and by 1955, not a single person over sixty is described as having a close relationship with a middle-aged or young adult. "Their destiny seems one of banishment to the 'senior citizen magazines,' " concludes Martel.

We support our own symbolic annihilation. Older women are the heaviest consumers of pulp romantic novels in which older women hardly appear. "They like nice romance and suspense, nothing too sexy. Harold Robbins, he's terrible! They prefer writers like Danielle Steele or Cynthia Freeman," I was told by a middle-aged salesperson in a book store. "He was a prominent surgeon, she was an international journalist," reads the blurb on the book cover, next to the ubiquitous picture of the tousled lass. And another: "A dazzling beauty, a dynamic award-winning executive, wife of a national TV anchorman, Samantha had the world on a string. Until the morning John told her he was leaving. She thought life was over, but it had barely begun. Suddenly she was torn between her high-powered career in New York and a life of raw, majestic freedom in California, aching for a rugged cowboy who promised her nothing but the irresistible passion of the moment." (Book jacket for *Palomino* by Danielle Steele.)

Neutered, annihilated people can only live vicariously—in fact, a series of these books marketed through chain drugstores is called, blatantly, Second Chance at Love.

Positive Countertrends

Symbolic annihilation, youth marketing, and stereotyping are our usual media fate. But there are also signs of hope.

To some degree, the media cannot help but reflect the graying of our population and the explosion of choices available to women today. In one hour's listening to my car radio I heard a fundamentalist preacher expounding on the "natural weakness" of women which keeps them dependent on men, then switched stations to a Salvadoran woman who was gathering support for her country, to Tish Sommers of the Older Women's League talking about legislative action for older women. And older women are benefiting from the groundswell of support for all minorities and subgroups. Gays, ethnic minorities, women, older people, the physically handicapped, etc., all are affirming their pride in who they are. Minority advocacy has become part of the fabric of our national life.

The media are responding to this trend by creating specialized programs, magazines, and books for these different audiences. Older women had tended to fall into the crack between *Ms.* and *Modern Maturity*. But in the last few years, the older women's movement has begun to remedy this situation.

For the first time we are coming out of the closet into the media, with the message "We exist." Although she's not totally realistic, we at least exist in the character of Mrs. Pynchon on the late *Lou Grant Show*. We exist in the series *Nurse*, in which Michael Learned plays an interesting middle-aged woman. We are writing about ourselves in publications like *Midmorphosis*, a San Francisco-based magazine with a national readership. Books like Lillian Rubin's *Women of a Certain Age* and Laurie Shields' *Displaced Homemakers* give us valuable information about our situation, and writers like Tillie Olsen, May Sarton, and Florida Scott-Maxwell convey our inner lives.

The older women's advocacy movement has made it a priority to promote the visibility of older women in the media. Just as Betty Friedan identified "the problem that has no name," thereby catalyzing the women's movement, Tish Sommers triggered a similar rush of recognition when she coined the phrase "displaced homemaker" to refer to the four million American older women who are "too old for men to care and too young for Medicare." One outcome was the founding of the Older Women's League, which lobbies and educates and publishes *OWL*, a newsletter with a media-watch service.

And the advertising business is suddenly becoming aware that an older people's market exists. A sudden flurry of articles has appeared in trade magazines like *Advertising Age* and *Business World*, saying in effect, "Hey, world, we have more old people in this country than young." Dr. Renee Frengut, president of Qualitative Decisions, a market research firm, confirmed the existence of this trend. "Why the advertising world has thought women cease to exist after forty-nine has always baffled me," she said. "And people over sixty have been completely ignored. But now there is a new awareness of the forty-to-fifty-five and the fifty-to-seventy-five-year-old market. My hunch is that you will see a shift to a more mature, more benefit-oriented, less frivolous and silly advertising. People have had it with the puffery."

Some of the most traditional older women's magazines like *Ladies' Home Journal*, *McCall's*, and *Good Housekeeping* have begun to depict working mothers, absent fathers, and premarital sex. These changes are based on readership surveys which reveal an important minority of "changing women."

New magazines like *Savvy* and *Working Woman* are being born. And magazines are changing. Where they used to ignore us, they now run articles telling us how to keep in shape. Kaylan Pickford, a stunning older model with gray hair, is a genuine ice breaker—the first older model who looks terrific, athletic—*and* her age.

And we can go to the movies and see "young" older women, like Jill Clayburgh, Diane Keaton, Jane Fonda, and Glenda Jackson, playing romantic leads—even with a few wrinkles! Although they're not truly older women, at least the age threshold has moved from the twenty-year-old to the forty-year-old. And Katharine Hepburn in *On Golden Pond* and Lila Kedrova in *Tell Me a Riddle* must be mentioned as unstereotyped and genuinely older women. But the most engaging middle-aged movie heroine to date is Dorothy, in Sydney Pollack's *Tootsie*—ironically played by Dustin Hoffman, a man.

Crazymaking

The media recognize that we are living in the 1980s. But quantitative analyses reveal that the powerful latent message to older women has not changed much. In spite of the women's advocacy movement, the new role models, and the with-it posture of the media, symbolic annihilation is the message with staying power, repeated ad nauseum but not articulated overtly.

We can scream from the housetops that older women exist, that wrinkles do not make sex impossible, that life over fifty consists of more than cleaning, cooking, and arthritis, but if our powerful media subtly contradict these statements, we are left in confusion.

As we have seen, tokenism can be the source of our confusion. Featuring one or two highly visible older women gives us the illusion, without the substance, of thoroughgoing change. This maneuver is called by feminist critics FW2, or "first women to . . ." It ignores the distance between the first woman to and the thousandth woman to. . . . Thus the few icebreakers like Barbara Walters and Kaylan Pickford should not make us too ecstatic, unless they are followed by many more like them. Women over forty are almost one-third of the female population, after all.

Another confusing media ploy is to co-opt new values in the service of the old goal: product sales. A perfect example is this Oil of Olay ad, which co-opts emerging positive attitudes toward women's maturity:

> Your husband reassures you that you've become much more interesting-looking over the years. And you recognize that, since your wedding, the mementoes of many emotions and the lingering traces of all those smiles have given your face the very special look of you. *And yet you'd still like to look younger than you do. It wouldn't be surprising if your more youthful look pleased him too.* [Italics added.]

And, by means of a "liberated" young woman, the Virginia Slims ads promote a product which actually *causes* wrinkles, illness, and death. Thus the old appeal to our fears is hooked into the new appeal to our pride.

The attention we are now getting in the women's magazines also has its crazymaking aspect. The message is: older women can now look and be like younger women, and isn't it terrific! *Harper's Bazaar* labels an entire issue "Over 40 and Sensational:

How to Look Younger Every Day." *Ms.* features a page called "Good News after 40 . . . 50 . . . 60 . . ." with pictures of Sophia Loren, Lauren Bacall, Jacqueline Onassis, and Elizabeth Taylor among others. Vicki La Motta at fifty-one is a *Playboy* centerfold. The upshot of this is the message: *you are now OK as an older woman, as long as you look like a younger woman.* This in fact reinforces the invisibility of most older women and keeps up the pressure to look young.

Age now means nothing, or almost nothing, these magazines continually say. They imply that we can all look like Audrey Hepburn or Shirley MacLaine if we follow the tips they give us. The grain of truth here is that it *is* possible and desirable to avoid lapsing into decrepitude. But these articles ignore the fact that these exceptional women have at their disposal time and money to maintain an illusion of youthfulness that are beyond the means of the average reader.

But if this average reader can be persuaded that passing for younger is the new norm, she will feel inadequate unless she too can do so—and thus she becomes the prey of the youth merchants (salon owners, cosmetics manufacturers, plastic surgeons), making sacrifices far beyond her means to keep up with the magic media mirror.

If we are the same as younger people, we should look the same, dress the same, follow the same fads (*Vogue* magazine: "The quickest way to appear older is not to be in fashion"). If we are the same as younger people and "age makes no difference," then presumably we will want to buy as many things as younger people do—plus all the things we will need to make us look like younger people.

This robs us not only of money but also of our peace of mind. Since we in fact know that we are not the same as younger women, we get the message that there is something wrong with us. We are told, "Be the same as younger women," not "Be yourself." This is no more a real liberation than a chemical that changes black skin into white would be an advance in the fight against racism. It is a sophisticated form of symbolic annihilation.

Resolving the Confusion

The media create a glossy, insubstantial image of women past forty and at the same time tell us subliminally over and over again that if we do not look like thirty-year-olds we are pitiful, boring, and inconsequential. This creates what the psychologist Gregory Bateson identified as a "double bind." In the double-bind situation, no matter what choice you make, you are wrong. Our thought processes have been muddled by all those unanalyzed images. When we try to think about our real problems, the glossy words and images are there below the level of consciousness, saying, "Things are fine." And when we think about our new feelings of power and hope, the process of symbolic annihilation leaves us again feeling "You are wrong—you don't even deserve to exist."

The truth is, things are probably worse *and* better for older women today. Rather than think we've made big advances, we are just beginning to see how vulnerable our gains are. The work against agism for women has just begun. The youth emphasis has never been so extreme, and the traditional safeguards such as marriage and alimony for women have never been so precarious. These real problems cannot be obliterated by not showing them on TV. As Lillian Rubin states: "For the vast majority of young women today, things will probably not be much better as they age. The 59 percent wage differential still holds, and if every woman were to use all her talent and brains and get paid accordingly, it would break the economy."

But on the other hand, Rubin herself is living witness of new possibilities. The context has shifted, particularly for better-educated, middle-class women, and the moral pressure for change has never been so clear. As we have seen, much of this pressure comes from our growing numbers. It would be ironic if the media responded to this fact by ending symbolic annihilation, only to make us visible as a new market for consumer goods—and nothing more.

We *are* feeling better about ourselves—at least some of us are. But these good feelings have been born of our struggles to make necessary changes in ourselves and in our society. True positive self-images are the outcome of such struggle.

It will take more than media events to make older women feel good about their lives. But the media could help. They could integrate us into all aspects of living in programming and advertising. They could show us using computers, modeling clothes, having love affairs, taking trips, drinking wine with friends, trying to make ends meet, giving expert advice about more than detergents. Or how about a prime-time show like the following?

"Cassie" is the name of a hypothetical new television pilot. Set in the Old West, it centers on the life experiences of its heroine, a 50-odd-year-old woman. Cassie is beautiful, lean, weathered, in excellent physical condition. Her hair is gray. She runs a large cattle ranch she has inherited from her deceased husband. She has several children. Men of all ages are attracted to her. Cassie is a complex person, both vulnerable and strong. Various episodes will show her teaching the ranch hands, mediating disputes with the Indians through her contact with Indian women, rescuing her first grandchild, enjoying the favors of a young ballad singer she befriends, learning healing from an old Indian woman, choosing to spend time riding in the desert alone, battling the mining company that threatens to destroy the town—and winning.

Cassie is not about to appear on next season's television roster. But if she did, she might become an ally in our struggle to overcome the double standard of aging.

7

BUYING YOUTH

Oh to be attractive. Oh to be attractive until they carry you out on a bier.

Violette Leduc, *La Bâtarde*

And the $8-billion-a-year beauty industry nods its agreement. Any doubts that we are more hung up on youth than ever should be dispelled by the amounts we spend to keep it—$6 million a day on products for the skin alone.

Beauty is youth; youth, beauty. In our culture the two are equated. As Dr. Renee Frengut, a market researcher, says: "When we sell a beauty product, we suggest that the product enhances beauty, which is the same in our society as enhancing youth." In a sense, then, all the exercise salons, facial salons, diet programs, cosmetics companies and beauty consultants, vitamins, shampoos, hair colorings—as well as the marketing of these—could rightly be considered part of the youth industry, although they have to do with health and beauty as well.

But despite the blurred boundaries between looking good and looking young, there are certain unequivocal hallmarks of aging. One of these—often the first to be noticed—is gray hair.

It used to be that only her hairdresser knew for sure, but today we dye and tell. Covering gray is almost totally accepted for both sexes. The so-called "bread and butter" browns and blacks that match most Americans' hair are the mainstay of the hair-coloring industry. But is this ubiquitous flight from gray really less peculiar than the eighteenth-century French custom of powdered wigs?

Covering gray is so simple and commonplace that there is no longer much emotional charge about it. When we think our more panicky thoughts about aging, the word that comes to mind is *skin.* Here feelings run higher, and procedures range from the simple and cheap to the complex and risky.

Our skin is nothing more or less than the wrapping for our self-esteem. Women in a nursing home who received a weekly facial, a morning application of cosmetics, and an evening cleansing showed a significant increase in self-esteem, as compared with women who didn't.

Our first line of defense is the bottles and jars. We buy oceans of lotions, cleansers, toners, exfoliants, pore refiners, masques, and gels. If all the creams were spread in one continuous layer, it would moisturize the Sahara.

We scrape our epidermis off with wire brushes. Or we burn it off with chemicals. Pregnant sheep and their unborn lambs are killed in faraway countries so that we can be injected with their hormones. We hook ourselves up to machines that make selected parts of our faces and bodies convulse forty times a minute. If we can afford it, we undergo major surgery on every part of our body above the knees to remove the offending flab.

Never before has the technology of youth been so sophisticated or sought after. Out of the welter of possible techniques, I will focus on the most common means at our disposal for turning back the clock—cosmetics and plastic surgery.

The consumers of these products and services are largely women, although men are increasingly involved. Myth has it that not only are men less interested in looking young, but that their skin actually does not age as fast as women's skin. This is not true.

Both men and women are equally subject to the three saboteurs of babyface smoothness: sun, gravity, and movement. But male skin is thicker than the skin of many (not all) women and has more underlying fat, at least until about the seventies. It also often contains more sebaceous glands, whose oily secretions mask (but do not prevent) wrinkle formation by keeping the skin hydrated. And the lower third of the male face is covered by the large hair follicles that comprise the beard. One dermatologist described the male face as a pegboard filled with plugs. "You can't pleat a pegboard," he said. For these reasons, male skin tends not to wrinkle but instead to form large folds and creases.

Our sexist and agist culture is more observing of the fine female wrinkles than of the large male folds. We define wrinkling as unattractive, while the male skin, comparably sun-damaged, drooping, and creased, will be perceived merely as weathered or interesting-looking. And all aging is thought to look worse on women anyway. If Walter Cronkite were female, we'd say he looked tired or old-looking. But nobody mistakes Walter's wattles for a lack of vitality. Even our perceptions are influenced by the double standard of aging.

To understand this, we first need to find out what aging of the skin actually is. This topic has not been a research priority, and little is actually known. Looking at skin under the microscope, however, can tell us certain things. In the first place, wrinkles, bags, and sags do *not* show up. What can be seen is that older people's skin is thinner. The bumpy projections of dermis into epidermis that characterize a young person's skin smooth out.

Sun damage, or elastosis, can also be seen. The dermis of my neck, for example, would be irregular and amorphous-looking microscopically, compared to the nicely patterned collagen bundles of my buttocks skin. To the naked eye, the neck skin would look blotchier and crepier. But skin also ages in two other ways. First, gravity's downward pull over the course of a lifetime results in drooping and wrinkling. Second, habitual movement patterns, such as frowning, squinting, and smiling, also leave their traces.

There is not too much you can do about movement wrinkles, except not move your face. This is seriously advocated in some circles. "Ever notice how stroke victims' faces smooth out on the affected side?" one doctor asked me. Most of us would find this to be going a bit too far. But we are told to break those nasty habits like squinting and frowning. The very thought makes me scowl. I can see what it does to my face—but what would *not* moving my face do to my soul? Some doctors actually cut the corrugator or frown muscle if we are inveterate frowners. But I still want mine; I reserve the right to frown if I feel like it.

Cosmetics

Much of the technology of cosmetics is aimed at providing the illusion of wrinkle-free skin. Creams substitute for natural skin oils by holding moisture in the upper layer of the epidermis to give a smoother appearance.

Today the average upper-middle-class family home contains $500 to $700 worth of beauty aids, according to market analysts. Does this estimate seem too high? Tally up all the shampoos, creme rinses, lipsticks used once and laid to rest in a drawer, half-used jars of cream, and the like. The figures mount quickly. Your teenage daughter may be using some of them to make herself look older. But I bet most of them have something to do with looking not only prettier but younger.

When we spend a dollar for cosmetics we are buying about eight cents' worth of product and ninety-two cents' worth of dreams. The markup on luxury creams can be astronomical. This year's magic formula, collagen, can sell for $200 a jar. It is certainly true that a jar of Estée Lauder has a more pleasant texture and a nicer package than a jar of Vaseline. And some moisturizers seem to hold moisture in the skin longer than others, making the skin *look* less wrinkled.

"There is some minimal difference between cheaper and better cosmetics," says dermatologist Sam Stegman. "The cheapest use heavier oils and then add soap systems and emulsifiers to make them feel good and spread well. These extra ingredients may irritate sensitive skins. Better cosmetics use more expensive oils. But there is nothing in a fifty-dollar cream that is not in a moderately priced one."

As for miracle ingredients, there is no evidence that any additives—repeat, *any*—from ginseng to collagen to elastin to turtle oil to royal jelly to hormones—do anything to retard aging. Nothing we can put on our skin retards aging. But too much sun, poor diet, stress, smoking, and lack of exercise can accelerate it.

The crazy thing is that we all know this. Anyone who has ever picked up a women's magazine has read the article by the eminent dermatologist who always gives us the same advice: stay out of the sun, keep your skin clean, use any cream you like. But turn the page and there is the column of new products, "results of scientific breakthroughs to arrest and even erase the ravaging effect of air, sunlight, time, on your skin." Not to mention all the advertisements on succeeding pages. The rational mind gives up in defeat.

Listening to cosmetics salespeople and salon operators confirms our vulnerability:

The great majority of women are searching for help. There's a lot of competition among women. You can sell them just about anything—they are very insecure.

Women are very sensitive about the aging of their skin. They say things like "All of a sudden I have these fine lines." They like euphemisms and don't like to use the word "wrinkles."

Women go way overboard—they do too much. I find that all the color, makeup, dyes we put on our faces and bodies does more harm than good to the skin. A man has his own coloring. A woman puts on foundation to put on rouge to match the color she had originally with nothing on her face.

As a group women are too obsessed with it all. They look in three-way mirrors every two minutes. Makeup should be a fun thing, it's not a Dostoyevskian type of problem if your lipstick doesn't exactly match your dress.

There is no way to stop the aging process, but you can age with grace. Certain women—it comes from inside—they never really age, because they have a relaxed, warm feeling. Men don't care, that's what makes them so interesting-looking later. But past fifty we have a ravaged, frightened, uptight look—we are frightened to death and show it all over.

One of the makeup models here had a face without a single line. Not one! But she never moved her face—it was horrible.

The crucial years start hitting in the late thirties—it works on 'em like all hell. Most of them are married to dudes that look at them like living room furniture. That's when they start to want the compliments, go for the hair dye—at that stage they'll pretty much go where you lead them. An older woman who wants attention is vulnerable. It's a hell of an age to be home popping popcorn by herself.

We know we are being had. But we don't want to dissect the cosmetics industry any more than a kid wants to get the drop on the Easter bunny. There are no Ralph Naders ready to take on the youth merchants. We *want* to pay fifty dollars for a face cream and we don't want to hear that the same cream is available for five dollars.

The youth doctors themselves tell us that they are frauds, but we won't listen. "I am not only a prostitute but a pimp," says Ivan Popov, the Yugoslavian who pioneered the use of such things as placenta and embryo extracts in cosmetics. And Ana Aslan, the mysterious Rumanian inventor of Gerovital procaine injections, says, "I'll give an individual who comes to me hope, even though they are hopeless and helpless, because I think it's cruel not to give them hope."

That cosmetics are 92 percent dreams is proven by the way they are marketed. Ad people and packaging people are already at work while the product is still being created. One could even say that the contents provide the pretext for the package. Most legal disputes between cosmetics firms are over theft of advertising ideas—not formulas. Everyone knows most products are alike, and the companies don't bother to try to prove otherwise; it's the package and sales gimmick that are hotly contested. And all the extensive testing of cosmetics is primarily to prove that the new "miracle" ingredients will boost sales without doing any harm— no one really expects them to do any good.

We underplay the role of cosmetics in our lives. "Did I put any makeup on today, I can't remember," says Jane with studied casualness as she bats her perfectly made-up eyes at me. "I barely look in the mirror—you know, just to drag a comb through my hair."

The ultimate artifice—and most subtle self-protection—is the "natural look." The following quotation from Katherine Pernitz's book, *Beyond the Looking Glass*, satirically tells us how to fool your man into thinking "he sees your naked face":

> Instead of the usual hour spent in making up, you need two. Each lash is applied individually. Every item—foundation, blusher, highlighter, shadow, eyeliner, mascara, eyebrow color, lipstick—must be used sparingly, must sink invisibly into the skin. The moment comes. Your freshly washed and set hair is loose and unsprayed. He enters. Your hands move up to cover your face (carefully) and you murmur, "You're so early! I haven't even had time to put on lipstick." He approaches, gently draws both hands away from the cherished face, contemplates a moment, then jubilantly announces, "Baby, you look great!"

As we get older, we often wear more makeup and feel "undressed" without it. "I have to put my face on," women used to say. The cosmetics may or may not actually hide wrinkles, but more important, they give us a psychological sense of cover and protection. We are not facing the world with the naked embarrassment of our aging skin. And we have all seen the extreme case of the older woman whose self-image is so negative or nonexistent that she literally paints on a youthful mask with which to "face" the world.

Using cosmetics involves not only time and money but also an element of risk. Hair dyes, perfumes, and certain coloring agents have been implicated as carcinogens. Any topical preparation (including those labeled hypoallergenic) can cause allergy or irritation in some people. Most of us are ready to take the gamble, but as we move from cosmetics to cosmetic surgery, we up the ante, financially, physically, and psychologically. We can use cosmetics and tell ourselves we only want to look better. But cosmetic surgery requires us to confront our stark desire to look younger, revealing how far we are willing to go to achieve this aim.

Cosmetic Surgery

Resorting to the knife is nothing new; once upon a time Cinderella's sisters hacked off hunks of their feet in order to interest the prince. Techniques have improved somewhat, but basic motivations haven't changed much.

Cosmetic surgery is growing in popularity. The New York City yellow pages, for example, list more than five times as many plastic surgeons as pediatricians. Men do it too, but according to professional estimates, 75 percent of all patients are female, widowed, divorced, or single and over forty. Ninety percent of the over-forties have suffered a major loss such as a death or a separation. In the forty- to fifty-year-old group, intense professional commitment, often with high public visibility, is common.

It is expensive. Prices start at about $2,000 for an eyelift. A full facelift is in the $5,000 to $6,000 range, with prices for body surgery often running even higher—and most of it not covered by medical insurance.

Cosmetic surgery fascinates me. I find it intriguing that we increasingly consider it normal to slice up our bodies and faces for purposes of rejuvenation. Every "how to" book for older women now takes it for granted as an option. But whether we view it as a godsend or a curious mutilation rite, we must admit that it epitomizes the double standard of aging.

Once you walk through the doors, and providing you have the cash up front, there are a number of different paths to the fountain of youth.

Dermabrasion, skin peeling, and injections, the least drastic of the cosmetic procedures, can be done by either dermatologists or surgeons. Dermabrasion and peeling are used to remove sun damage. They are painful procedures, chemical peeling particularly. The peeled client looks awful for two weeks and pinkish red for months thereafter. She must stay out of the sun for months, preferably forever. If done clumsily, or on the wrong kind of skin, the new skin can emerge with areas of strange shininess, depigmentation, or a telltale line of demarcation. Peeling prices range from $1,000 to $3,000.

Injections of small amounts of either liquid silicone or collagen are used to plump out small wrinkles. Liquid silicone is controversial to use, illegal to sell. It is long lasting but sometimes ends up in the wrong place over time. Collagen injection, a newer procedure, lasts six to eight months; it causes occasional allergic reactions. These procedures cost in the hundreds.

There are many cosmetic surgery procedures, but the eyelid lift, or blepharoplasty, and the face lift, or rhytidectomy (literally "wrinkle remover"), are by far the most common. Next in popularity are body contouring operations, like the various breast reshaping operations—augmentation, reduction, and mastopexy, or breast lift. Abdominoplasties remove the loose, striated skin which often results from multiple pregnancies. The upper arms can also be deflabbed and the hands dewrinkled. (And while you are at it, age spots can be frozen off or removed chemically.) Saddlebags can be removed from the outer thighs, flab from the inner thighs. The buttocks can be lifted and reshaped. All these operations address the effects of gravity on the face and body.

Body-contouring surgery is perhaps the most blatant proof of the desperation with which we seek youth. The trade-off we make is long, unsightly scars for flab. Even with the best technique in the world, the heavy skin on the body heals with obvious scarring—and if we are lucky that is all that will happen. "These tissues do not heal kindly," says the *Atlas of Aesthetic Plastic Surgery*. All the doctor can do, if he does well by us, is locate the scars where they will not show. (The "before" pictures in the texts are nude; the "afters" are wearing bikinis.)

Body surgery is serious business. General anaesthesia must be used. Complications are not unusual, and recovery time is the same as for other major surgery. Some plastic surgeons take a dim view of these operations, but the laws of supply and demand ensure that others will be ready and willing. One text talks about the high risks obese patients run, and then adds, "However, the aesthetic results must be weighed against the morbidity [illness]." Nor does the possibility of death deter some.

Make no mistake. We are asking for these operations. "Most patients feel so self-conscious about their appearance that they will spend a tremendous amount of time putting themselves through major surgery so they can feel better about themselves." Another text states: "Trading the excess skin for an incredible scar seems to be a reasonable trade-off," adding that the number of persons seeking body contouring is rapidly increasing.

Complications and Credulity

It is not the fault of doctors that operations have complications. Living tissue is being traumatized; how it will heal is never totally predictable. An incision can look great at first and then pucker as it heals. Thick scars called keloids can form. Infection is always a possibility, greater in some areas of the body than others.

Facial surgery is considered a low-risk procedure. The possible complications are bleeding (clots in the tissue or the bloodstream), injury of sensory or motor nerves (temporary or permanent), skin perforation, infection, flap necrosis (the dying of the lifted skin), scarring, earlobe misplacement, hair loss, death (from a clot migrating to the lungs), blindness (from bleeding behind the eyes), too much white of eye showing, inability to close eyes (from overzealous tissue removal or healing contracture). None of these complications is really rare, and death reports from facial surgery reach the L.A. County medical examiner's office at the rate of one every six to eight weeks.

Reading the doctors' own words can be a sobering experience. The literature talks about the "disintegration of the high standards of plastic surgery training and responsibility to the welfare of patients." Another text warns: "Multiple wrongly placed scars of the uncaring surgeon have created permanent deformities. The misuses of outpatient surgery for problems for which hospitalization is a basic requirement has resulted in the most dire consequences."

"Rarely do we hear much in the way of a negative report, or a refutation of an earlier glowing account of an operating procedure," states Ross H. Musgrave in a cautionary presidential address to the Association of Plastic and Reconstructive Surgeons. This statement recalls the former widespread use of liquid silicone, a procedure that now has become an embarrassment to the profession. And Thomas Rees, a leading plastic surgeon, asked at a conference, "I would like to poll the audience and ask how many have seen a permanent paralysis resulting from injury to the frontal or temporal branch of the facial nerve after face-lifting. Yes, I see by the response that others also have seen it happen. I have seen a number of cases in my office." And another panelist replies, "I guess I have been lucky. I will have to be more careful."

I stress the dark side of the surgical picture because, according to doctors, women notoriously gloss over it. All reputable physicians want informed consent for any procedure. They are therefore careful to talk about the risks involved, but we don't absorb this information.

According to one text: "Once she finds out something can be done, she perpetuates in total blind trust, surrendering herself completely and putting the physician in charge." And it goes on to say, "The patient has no fear of the risks that she is taking with her healthy body. The term 'tummy tuck,' which is frequently used by women's magazines, becomes implanted in the patient's mind and gives her the illusion that the surgery is a minor one. The idea of complications or death rarely occurs to any patient . . . the patients were found to have total dependence on the physician, whom they believed to be infallible."

Several studies showed that patients screen out doctors' warnings. One study of twenty women who were carefully informed revealed that only three remembered as many as three complications! "It won't happen to me," "It's not my time," "I heal well," "I take vitamin C," "I picked the right doctor," "I take care of myself," were some of the rationalizations given.

This tendency to deny the danger is upsetting to ethical surgeons. However, three researchers explain that it is a necessary precondition for surgery. "Surprisingly, many patients are totally unaware that postoperative complications are an inescapable consequence of any operation," write Drs. Marcia and John Goin and Rodney Burgoyne. "If they heard and truly believed that there was a real possibility they might develop facial paralysis as a result of an elective esthetic procedure, they could hardly allow themselves the indulgence of something they want very much."

A level-headed evaluation of risks is made more difficult by the way cosmetic surgery is described. Both laypersons' and doctors' language tends to obscure, in different ways, the fact that a normal, healthy body is being cut into. *Cosmo* trills: "Aren't you curious about what's new in nose, bosom, and derrière bobs? It's time to have that straighter nose, trimmer tum." All the talk about "tummy tucks" and "nose bobs" is calculated to make us feel as if we are not living tissue, but dress fabric.

Medical talk takes a different tack. By giving normal conditions medical labels, the doctors find it easier to believe that their services are medically indicated. Small breasts are "micromastia." "The patient presenting with micromastia is the ideal candidate for mammary implantation." In other words, if your breasts are small and you want implants, you can have them.

Plastic surgeons call everything they don't like a "deformity." Aging is called "aging deformity" or "atrophic deformity." And you don't have a fat pad on your thigh, you have "trochanteric lipodystrophy." After two days in the library, I began to wonder how I had survived for so long without plastic surgery.

Marketing Youth

With the aging of our population, youth becomes an increasingly salable commodity. Plastic surgeons shape this demand by articulating a particular standard of beauty which dovetails with women's fear of aging.

The surgeons get their standards the same way the rest of us get them—from the media. Lauren Hutton's eyes were instantly recognizable in a medical textbook as examples of the standard to be emulated:

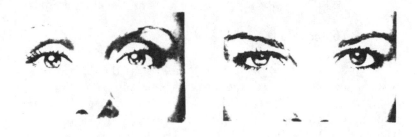

The text stresses the value of the attractive "Caucasian" appearance of the model's eyelids. And the *Atlas of Aesthetic Plastic Surgery* states, "In order for the breast to be aesthetically pleasing, it should be a relatively firm, full breast which stands out from the chest wall and states with certainty: 'I am feminine.' "

Besides expecting breasts to talk, the surgeons are not bashful about suggesting additional operations to bring us up to snuff. In my opinion, it is one thing to tell someone her gall bladder needs to come out, and quite another to say her jowls need to come off. There is no objective need for any cosmetic surgery, but many doctors create demand by putting the weight of their authority behind their personal aesthetic judgment.

"Doing the eyelids is like slip-covering a chair—it makes the rest of the room look tired," said one doctor. And the literature is casual about recommendations for thighplasty and mastopexy when a patient comes in for an abdominoplasty ("tummy tuck"). One woman told me:

I went for an eye lift and the doctor said, "You certainly could use a face lift too."

"I like my face," I told the doctor. "It's my neck I'm not sure about."

"I have to do your face to do your neck, and I'll do your eyes too. In ten years you'll appreciate it," he said. "It is customary to do the eyes at the same time as the face," the doctor told me.

I said I didn't think I needed my eyes done—so he pulled my eyelid out with a pair of tweezers and it kinda hung out there.

"You could use it," he said.

Even so, we are not always as compliant as the doctors would like. "You sometimes see the result of noncompliance," said one. "If I tell them they need not only a face lift but also a face peel, or they need their upper lip dermabraded, as well as peeling around the eyes, and they don't do it, the poor result is not the doctor's fault. Of course, the patient may have a limited amount of money," he added.

One doctor showed me "befores" and "afters" of his face peelings. The photographs were excellent, usually profiles seen at very close range. I was struck in the "before" pictures by the beauty of the wrinkles, as they followed the contour of the bones. I was looking at human landscapes that recalled sand dunes and desert rocks. These faces had what used to be called character—a most nonmarketable beauty. (Yes, the "after" pictures did look younger.)

I left the doctor's office filled with sadness as I thought about the pressures that drive us to subject our faces to a second-degree burn—a "horrendous procedure" in the words of the doctor himself.

The Face Lift

The archetypal rejuvenating operation is the face lift. Two million were done last year, and candidates are getting progressively younger. Carole, a French designer, told me, "I have the kind of face that shows aging already, even though I'm only thirty-five. Why should I not look my best? The surgeon showed me he could just fix it here and here [she pulls up her skin at her temples to show me] and I looked fresher, not so tired."

Doctors recommend getting an early start. One writes, "It seems that the longer a patient waits to have the primary rhytidectomy, the more likely he or she is to develop early recurrence of the deformity. I believe it is advantageous to do the initial procedure at a relatively early age, such as in the fourth or even the third decade, if indicated." (The "deformity" referred to is, of course, aging of the face.)

Successive operations are also advised: "The patient who wants to look as good two years later as he or she did three months after primary rhytidectomy should be told that an early secondary operation will be needed. The secondary face lift may be expected to hold up longer than the first operation. Subsequent renewal operations can then be done at progressively longer intervals. Patients who wish to 'fix' their ages might benefit from a second renewal operation three to four years later and perhaps even a third renewal operation five to seven years after the second one."

In certain circles face lifts are a status symbol. The Palm Beach crowd talks about Dr. X's and Dr. Y's faces—as if they were comparing brands of designer jeans. "I went to a convention in Chicago," one plastic surgeon told me, "and all the women in the lobby looked alike. I thought I had stumbled into *The Stepford Wives* or something. They all had the same noses, 'lifts' from the same schools of work, chin implants. They were all perfectly made up, beautifully dressed. At first I didn't get it—then I realized they were the doctors' wives." (I bet all the doctors didn't look alike, though.)

Motivations for Cosmetic Surgery

Some research implies that you have to be a little crazy to want cosmetic surgery. Body-contouring clients, in particular, are described as frequently having "distortions of self-image, concept, and worth." Another study claims that these clients have higher rates of psychotic illness than do face lift clients.

But faceliftees do not get off scot-free either. One text reports that they are "perfectionistic," "having an intense commitment to their jobs with deliberately distorted personal relationships," or as "dealing with an underlying depression by denial or activity, mechanisms that are threatened by aging." The vast majority are said to "seek the operation on the basis of unrealistic or distorted motivations."

Of course there are surgery junkies, who want every part of themselves fixed and who are never satisfied. They are clearly in need of psychological rather than surgical help. But I would tend to feel that the clinical picture cited above is somewhat hard on women.

If we *are* crazy to cut ourselves up to look younger, it is also crazy to have to live in a culture which penalizes aging. According to surgeons, there is only one acceptable motivation for cosmetic surgery: to look better for yourself. I would say this constitutes an unrealistic expectation on the part of the surgeon. Life for single older women being what it is, I am not surprised that women want face lifts for a whole raft of reasons, realistic and unrealistic.

Women are aware, however, that only certain motivations are considered acceptable. They know their doctor does not want to be held responsible if the super job or super man does not materialize. So we have two sets of explanations: the private set (which we are sometimes not really in touch with ourselves) and the set for doctor and/or public.

An interesting study in which twenty women were interviewed before and after surgery found "the virtual omnipresence of a hidden agenda." Preoperatively, the women's motivations were pragmatic—getting rid of sagging skin, looking better, eliminating that tired look, and so forth. After the operation, intensive interviews revealed the following motivations: hope that the operation would make them feel physically younger, fear of narrowing of options due to aging, desire for involvement with younger people, desire for sexual freedom, to cure husbands' impotence, to get a better job, to compete with a sixteen-year-old daughter, fear of dying, wanting to stay young for a young husband, not wanting problems to show, not wanting to appear bitter, since "old people look bitter."

When I asked, the first reason most women gave to me for surgery was simply not liking the signs of age. But they certainly had the withdrawal of male attention in the back, if not the front, of their minds. This did not surprise me. However, when sixty-year-old Charlotte, whose scars were still fresh, pulled a life-size cardboard-backed photograph of her (married) lover out from under her bed, I was a little taken aback. "My life has revolved around men," she said. "I've never been more than two or three weeks between men. I'm really quite terrified about facing the future by myself—I hate the thought!"

Charlotte may be extreme, but she is not alone. My interviews with women who had had face lifts always seemed to lay bare their need for men and their fear of solitude. The nakedness of the dependency feelings expressed was hard to listen to. "All I have to do is meet the right man and it will be all right" was a comment I heard frequently.

> My times without a man are always despairing, anxiety-ridden. I feel I'll *never* have another man. It's pathetic, isn't it? Fifty-two years old and still waiting for Mr. Right.

However, most women were ambivalent about wanting the surgery, even when not ambivalent about the results:

> I bought it—the whole shtick. I listened to too many love songs, saw *Gone With the Wind* five times—and all those commercials saying you have to be beautiful, young, seductive.

> I'm very pleased with the surgery—but I haven't mentioned the other side of this. Why am I trying to look better for the auction block? My mother had a meat-on-the-market point of view. She was sensational-looking, like an actress. I'm afraid I absorbed a lot of her point of view.

> Why does a person have to be pretty? A pretty woman doesn't develop the way an ugly woman might—she's gotten undeserved attention all her life.

It's an awful thing they did to us—making us feel we can't look natural.

To me these women were magnifying mirrors for feelings many of us must also own up to. But you don't have to be unusually dependent to want a lift. I have interviewed many women who struck me as perfectly well balanced. They simply wanted to have their faces going for them in the economic and sexual marketplace.

I got a face lift as part of my re-entry strategy after my divorce. I was having trouble getting credentialed for my job—I'm a learning-disabilities teacher—and I knew I would face tremendous competition from younger people. It was part of a campaign to pay more attention to my clothes, my body, to lose a little weight. I went out and spent a thousand dollars on clothes then, too. It was the first time in my life I ever did anything like that.

I know that without physical beauty—if men don't get that first "hit"—they disregard you. So I felt this was something I needed to do.

Whatever the reasons they gave, women who elected to have surgery shared the assumption "I want to be my age but not look it." We are too naked, somehow, with our bare faces hanging out. We don't want to show the traces of pain—as well as joy. We believe that we cannot both look our age and look good. And we don't identify with our faces as we age. We become the "Other" to ourselves, while inside we retain an image from the past as the "real" us.

But not everybody feels this way. Some people don't want to do it and don't like the way it looks. A psychologist friend said:

Their eyes look so helpless behind those drawn-back faces—they can't express what they want to express anymore. Audrey Hepburn is a perfect example. She looked so wonderful as

Maid Marian—she had wrinkles—now she is absolutely skinny and cannot move her face.

And he added:

If you have seen enough of them you start to notice subtle things—like the wrinkles that go the wrong way when certain expressions cross their faces. And there is a certain lack of "match" between the face and other parts of the body.

And C. W. Gusewelle, writing in the *San Francisco Chronicle* under the headline "The Attraction of Experienced Women," says:

As the years have passed, I have come to find more attraction in women who have lived long enough to display a moderate amount of weathering. But what has helped clarify my feelings on the matter has been, oddly enough, a new-found amateur interest in the lapidary art—the search for beauty in stones. . . . To discover it, one needs a machine called a tumbler. . . . The pebbles are put inside, many of them at once, and the barrel of the tumbler turns, driven by a small motor. . . . The process cannot be hurried. In revealing beauty, there is no substitute for time. . . . But when finally the pebbles are taken from the tumbler and cleaned, they are found to be lastingly transformed. Drying does not dull them anymore. Their luster is permanent. Fractional layers have been ground away. So that what seemed, at the first, to be minor imperfections are accentuated and made clearer, becoming now lines and swirls arranged in patterns of considerable beauty.

Results and Rituals

Is it worth it? That depends on whom you ask. There is no question that some women do look younger as a result of cosmetic surgery—but not as dramatically as I would have thought. Our obsession with the wrinkle tends to obscure the fact that what counts most is the overall "gestalt" we present. This "gestalt" is a function of many factors, like posture, muscle tone, weight, energy level, and mood.

A sagging chinline can be nipped and tucked, it is true. Or the neck which supports it can be kept supple and elongated. The neck and face muscles, like any other muscles of the body, can be kept in tone. We are not as dependent on the knife as we may think. But we lack this kind of education, and we rely on medical solutions to our problems.

Even when results are totally satisfactory, a faceliftee must face the fact that the aging process continues, and many of the feelings that it triggers come back to haunt them. "I am now developing frown lines again," said Joanne. "Yes, I would go back again for another operation. All this business for me ultimately has to do with immortality—with staving off the grim reaper. I am a happy person, I don't want to be depressed, I'm an 'up' type of person . . ." She broke off and turned away.

Most of us realize that surgery cannot be the final solution. The problems of older women in our society are more than skin deep. After a face lift, Prince Charming and the good job often remain as elusive as ever. Yet women are overwhelmingly delighted with their operations. The question is, why?

Even the surgeons seem bemused by their resounding success. "In a statistical survey of results," writes one physician, "the psychological failures are easily identified, whereas the successful results included a mixture of realistic and magical cures which are hard to differentiate."

The simplest answer is that women are just happier to look younger, or think they look younger. "I love the compliments," "It gave me a lift," "I love to pass the mirror and see my face now" were typical comments.

But there is more to it than that. I believe cosmetic surgery *as a process* fills a gap in our culture. I had been saying for years, "Why do we have rituals for all other events in our lives but the midlife passage? We badly need a menopause ritual."

Cosmetic surgery has all the earmarks of a rite of passage. It is usually undertaken at a time of transition. As in primitive tribes, a sacrifice must be made. The ritual involves a period of withdrawal. There are ordeals to endure with courage: the facing of pain, social disapproval, possible medical complications. The anesthesia and analgesia produce an altered state of consciousness. There are scarification ceremonies. And the doctor is the shaman who leads us through it all.

And then we emerge—cleansed of the past, reborn. And we are welcomed back, nurtured, complimented. No wonder that women seem so unconcerned about the expense and risks involved—these only heighten the meaning of the event. But how ironic that in our culture the midlife rite of passage leads—backward.

"Beauty" and "Youth" Are Not Synonyms

My anti-lift bias is clear, yet I would not condemn any woman who wants one. I understand the pressures on us too well. But there are alternatives to explore before choosing surgery.

It is true that we cannot change the eyes of others. But we can change our own. Destroying the double standard of aging *in ourselves* may not change the world overnight, but it will make *us* feel better. And it will make us feel more compassion for each other. The grooves in our psyches left by all those years of reading *Cosmo* and seeing *Gone With the Wind* five times are more damaging to us than any lines in our faces.

This will involve considerable inner reprogramming. We can start with the realization that "beauty" and "youth" are not synonyms. There is a distinction between looking older and looking ugly, depressed, ill, tired, or out of shape. Absence of wrinkles makes you look young. But good posture, appropriate weight for one's frame, and decent muscle tone of face and body are more important—and are achievable goals, possibly forever. (The next chapter will discuss some of these alternative approaches to well-being and good looks.)

Looking older, in fact, can mean looking radiantly healthy in a seasoned, interesting way. The French word *distingué* comes to mind. It means distinguished—literally, different from the others. Think of how similar all babies look. Life is a process of individuation, and it shows. Look about you for examples of mature women who capitalize on the uniqueness they have achieved in the course of a lifetime, and take them to heart.

Then do some reprogramming with your own mirror. Try looking at yourself as if you had never seen a copy of *Vogue*. Think about all your good qualities—especially the ones you didn't have at age thirty. Notice how they have been recorded on your face and body, and *appreciate* this. Then think about the beauty of your youth, acknowledge it, and let it go. See if you can begin to accept your face and body *now* as *you*.

And go back to the mirror again. Don't expect your attitudes to change overnight. Enlist the support of other women. Talk it out; encourage this change of attitude among one another.

Using other women for support makes sense because this is a group problem. Face-lifting is essentially an individual solution to this group problem, but as such it has certain effects on the group.

It puts women who do not have the time and money to spend on cosmetic surgery at a disadvantage. The look of a naturally aging female face is becoming increasingly not normal-looking. After all, our tastemakers are, by and large, lifted these days. Could the President's wife get by without it anymore, I wonder? This means that the woman without $5,000, or the woman who chooses to take that $5,000 and spend it on a year of college for her daughter, begins to look increasingly deviant from what is considered good-looking in our society.

I am disturbed by this competitive pressure on women. It has been a feature of our democratic culture that anyone can dress tastefully and be stylish, even on a moderate budget. But there are no popular-price face lifts. The gap between the haves and the have-nots thus becomes plain as the nose on your face.

Nevertheless, there still may be things about your looks you decide you cannot live with. If you think you want surgery, don't beat yourself up about it. It is not a crime. What is criminal is the system that fosters it. But do go to a medical library and look at some actual pictures of operations. This is guaranteed to banish any lingering illusions that cosmetic surgery is a panacea. Then if you are still convinced that the benefits outweigh the disadvantages for you, your next task is to find the right surgeon.

Choosing a Surgeon

This may not be easy. First of all, the demand for cosmetic surgery exceeds the supply of well-trained people. Any M.D. is legally entitled to perform any type of surgery, and cosmetic surgery is a tempting option for doctors with questionable credentials.

In addition, we often complicate this search by the way we go about it. If we need knee surgery, we go to a doctor we trust for a recommendation, or we call our local medical board. But when we shop for a cosmetic surgeon, we may go to the yellow pages or answer ads in magazines. Perhaps we are ashamed to tell our doctor that we want cosmetic surgery. Besides, we may not trust his opinion, with some justification. Medicine, not aesthetics, is probably his strong point. But you want someone who will not harm you, and will *also* make you look good. The vast majority of unpleasant consequences of surgery are not life-threatening but aesthetic: asymmetries, poorly shaped breasts, too tight faces, and so forth.

If it were my body, I would want to check and cross-check both the medical and aesthetic credentials of the surgeon. No one reference is foolproof. To begin with, he should be subject to the review of his peers, therefore on the staff of a major hospital.

Ask dermatologists and other skin-care professionals. Call your local medical society and get some names and go talk to several doctors. Don't be fooled by pretty pictures. A dead giveaway of questionable practice is the doctor who presents his book of photographs as any kind of proof. Changes of lighting and angle can easily create the illusion of vast improvement even when there is none. And his boo-boos will not be in the book.

If you are not sure, go back and get some more names. If

friends recommend someone, check his credentials. You can also contact the American Society of Plastic and Reconstructive Surgeons. Their address is 29 E. Madison Street, Suite 800, Chicago, Ill. 60602.

The appeal of surgery is easy to understand. In this uncertain world, the one thing it may seem we have control over is our own bodies. As for me, there were days when I was tempted. But as I do my mirror meditation today, I realize that I like what my face has become. I could no longer conceive of it without its wrinkles. Anyone who is going to take me on is going to have to take on all of me, I'm afraid—with a full complement of years and the signs of their passage.

8

"WOMEN'S COMPLAINTS"

Nagging, overweight and premature aging are the outward signs of misery, and they are so diffuse among women in our society that they do not excite remark. Women feel guilty about all of them: they are the capital sins of "letting yourself go."

Germaine Greer, *The Female Eunuch*

Disowning Our Bodies

In spite of our efforts to shape, adorn, shrink, rejuvenate, and otherwise control them, we do not possess our bodies. We have long since relinquished them. In all of these efforts we are merely acting as executors of the will of others, the Significant Others, who have let us know from childhood what a woman's body should be. As a result, by the time we are older, we are not at home in our bodies—if we ever were before. Our bodies no longer lend themselves to our pliant manipulation. By becoming older, our bodies develop a will of their own; they change in ways that we, acting as agents of the culture, do not want them to change. And so we retaliate against this betrayal by disowning them. No longer our bodies at all, they feel like alien shells that imprison us.

And yet we cannot truly disown them, because we *are* our bodies. We can try to ignore this fact, but this is not too successful a strategy. We can run away from many unpleasant experiences, but how can we run from our own bodies? They are doing the running.

As women, we know that this is true. Our language confirms it; we know it in our bones, our hearts, our guts. We know that our most powerful experiences have taken place in our bodies, through our bodies—such as lovemaking, giving birth. In fact, if we reflect at all, we realize that the major part of our experience— good and bad—takes place in our bodies. Even the excitement of a new idea is only experienced because it stimulates physical responses. Our breathing subtly quickens, our muscles cause us to sit up and take notice, our eyes open wider.

And, of course, every emotion comes to us as a physical state and leaves its effects. We don't really know how. But we do know that if you think you are "too old" for bicycling, college, or love, the body will oblige and make this true.

Even though all life is lived through the body, the male norm is to minimize its importance. Men pride themselves on their imperviousness to pain and other feelings. Even though they too grow, suffer, have moods, and get old, they conceive of their physical life as basically continuous and unnoticeable. This idea of a body as immutable is seen as natural and desirable, although all of nature, with its fluctuations and cycles, tells us otherwise.

The grim continuity of work life—with its eight-hour days and forty-hour weeks ad infinitum—makes the "messy," unpredictable female body seem deviant. We too share this male norm and try to approximate it. We apologize for our bodies. But this is not everywhere the case. Most nonindustrial cultures recognize female periodicity and accommodate to it. What if we too could experience our discontinuities of menstruation, pregnancy, and menopause not as inconveniences to be minimized, but as opportunities to reestablish our connection with nature? Perhaps men, too, would profit from a few days' official R & R each month, sitting in the equivalent of a menstrual hut!

Instead, we accommodate to the male norm and make our bodies "wrong"—particularly where aging is concerned. And believing that decreptitude is just around the corner makes it happen. Bodies that are despised and disowned take their revenge.

"Women's Complaints"

We may, in fact, aid and abet this bodily revolt. Until very recently, we were powerless to overtly challenge the double standard of aging; what's more, we did not even acknowledge its unfairness. Illness, then, was the one permissible way to voice the "female complaints" that our mouths did not dare to utter. In this way, we gained a measure of redress and attention:

My mother was in perpetual menopause. She always explained her behavior that way. Always resented the life forced on her—felt she had no choice.

I have a friend who has back pain at fifty-one. The doctor told her she was starting menopause, that there was nothing she could do. Well, now she's got her husband and children all walking softly around her, telling them she's going through a difficult time and needs extra consideration.

The female role itself predisposes us to sickness. Although the Victorian woman with her vapors is a thing of the past, to be vaguely indisposed—physically or emotionally—is still considered woman's lot. Although we see doctors no more frequently than men do, apart from our ob-gyn visits, the line between sick and healthy is blurred for women. In a much-quoted psychological study, the Brovermans found that personality traits such as dependency, emotionalism, passivity, narcissism, and subjectivity were rated as normal for women and also as "less healthy," while the profile of the mentally healthy person corresponded with the male cluster of traits: independence, aggressiveness, dominance, activity, adventurousness. The Brovermans conclude: "For a woman to be healthy, from the adjustment viewpoint, she must adjust to and accept the behavioral norms for her sex, even though these behaviors are considered less healthy."

Illness, both physical and mental, in women can be considered an exaggeration of traits that in their milder forms are considered to be normal female behavior. Thus women who are deeply dissatisfied with their role have two options: to leave the role and be considered less feminine, or to exaggerate the role and become frankly sick.

In fact, mental illness is disproportionately female, just as criminality (an exaggeration of "normal" male traits) is disproportionately male. Women report twice as much personal discomfort and symptoms consistent with mental illness. We represent about two-thirds of hospitalized depressives, psychoneurotics, and schizophrenics. And aging and mental illness in women go together, according to Phyllis Chesler:

> In terms of age, 20 to 34 are women's "prettiest" and child-bearing years. Even if they are "unhappy" or functioning at low levels, their childbearing responsibilities and/or sexually youthful appearance keep them within the "outside" patriarchal institutions such as marriage and private psychotherapy. The largest number of women in both general and private hospitals are between the ages of 35 and 44. White and/or wealthy women in private hospitals, black and/or poor women in general psychiatric wards are reacting to being both overworked and paradoxically, to the beginning signals of their sexual and maternal "expendability." . . . State and county asylums function as a final dumping ground for "old" women. Thirty-two percent of the total female population incarcerated in state and county hospitals in 1968 were over 65.

Female complaints, not surprisingly, show up in the workplace as well. Elizabeth Janeway writes that "epidemics of stress" sweep through plants where boring, repetitive work with high noise levels is the rule. This sort of job, says Janeway, is often held by a woman who needs the work badly and who puts up with it because she lacks training. So-called hysterical symptoms like headaches, dizziness, visions of blue mists, perceptions of bad smells and tastes . . . are promptly picked up and shared. Hence epidemics.

The sharing is important. The problem may still be defined as "hysteria," but if half a factory floor is hysterical, management gets the idea that something ought to be done about it. In fact, the old diagnosis is now passé, and the National Institute for Occupational Safety and Health has begun to look for external causes. A clinical psychologist, Michael Colligan, who is attached to the Institute, suggests that the women who suffer from such "psychogenic" illnesses are, quite simply, making a statement about their situation: "This place makes me sick."

The "job" of older woman also seems to make us sick. The number of female-related disorders associated with midlife is striking. Perhaps this is solely due to the sheer complexity of the female reproductive system. But these organs are also the logical targets for our hidden feelings about the unsatisfactory "working conditions" that go with the "job."

Breast cancer occurs in one out of every ten women. Incidence plateaus between forty-two and forty-seven, and then begins a slow steady ascent in the early fifties. Uterine problems like prolapse, fibroid tumors, cancer, endometriosis, and pelvic inflammatory disease are partly responsible for the fact that hysterectomy is the most common operation performed in the United States today. Vaginal infections are also extremely common, especially among older women. And menopause often brings with it a host of difficulties.

Menopause

Otherwise called the climacteric, from the Greek *klimaktér* meaning "top rung of the ladder," menopause reveals the complex way that our culture affects our bodies. The top rung of the ladder is a privileged spot—a jumping-off place to a new level. Cross-cultural studies indicate that in many traditional societies, the status of women rises dramatically after menopause. Postmenopausal women function as midwives, matchmakers, conductors of ceremonies, and healers. The Bengali woman is no longer in purdah, and obtains the keys to the kitchens and storerooms, symbolizing her command and authority. In traditional China, the older woman wielded tremendous power over her sons and daughters-in-law who resided with her. Not surprisingly, menopausal problems are rare in China. And anthropologist Estelle Fuchs states that some Welsh women believe that hot flashes carry them quickly and safely through the menopause. Among these women, *not* to have them is embarrassing, and they sometimes complain that they are "not very good at it."

It must be noted, however, that this new power is usually contingent upon neutering. An exception was the Blackfoot Indians, among whom "Old Lady" was a term of respect. The so-called "manly hearted" women among them were not masculine but were older wives, passionately sexual and especially favored.

In our society, of course, the situation is reversed. Youth is prime time and menopause is perceived as a kind of death. (It once was, in fact, a precursor of death, since few women lived much beyond menopause until after the turn of the century.)

In any given society, the status of fertile women is reversed at menopause. Where young women are honored and prized, older women are denigrated, and vice versa. It would seem that no society has yet managed to give women a respected place throughout their lives.

Menopause is a profound shift, socially, psychologically, and physiologically, though it need not be a negative one. However, for about 10 percent of women, the discomforts of hot flashes and vaginal dryness are very real and upsetting. But we are expected to minimize it, as we are expected to minimize our other female processes—except for the ones that directly give men pleasure. The French writer Annie LeClerc deplores this belittling of women's bodily experience. She celebrates women's sexual life, which she defines broadly. "What should I call my periods, my pregnant belly, my milk, if not aspects of my sexuality—what should I call all that I experience through them and by means of them, if not sexuality?" And she adds, "While we are not reconciled with ourselves, and first of all with our bodies, we will be slaves and accomplices in the oppressive triumph of a virile, disenchanted world." But even LeClerc ignores menopause as another episode in the unfolding of a woman's sexual life. Like so many other writers, she allows this experience to remain shrouded in silence and shame.

Since most of our data comes from people seeking help, not too much is known about normal menopause. It has been estimated that 10 percent of women report severe menopausal difficulties, that another 10 percent report no symptoms, and that the bulk of women make this transition with only minimal problems. Some postmenopausal women talk about PMZ, or postmenopausal zest, a feeling of great serenity and vigor that arrives once the throes of the reproductive cycle are past.

Yet we are still apprehensive about it, particularly if we are younger women. Sociologist Bernice Neugarten found great variation in women's expectations of what menopause would bring. This uncertainty about what to expect troubles many women more than the actual symptoms.

Fortunately, many good books on the market today address these fears by providing detailed information and support (see the list of titles at the end of the next chapter). Yet the very existence of so many "menopause manuals" attests to the fact that we still view it as a problem and a leading "women's complaint."

Emotional Problems: Depression

Another "complaint" often associated in the public mind with menopause is depression. It has been described as a female epidemic, affecting three times as many women as men. Like other women's complaints, it is a way of turning frustration and anger inward, against the self, instead of directing it outward. It should come as no surprise that it is more prevalent among homemakers than among career women. In fact, according to sociologist Pauline Bart, depression in older women and acceptance of the traditional female role go hand in hand.

The key experience in depression is loss. Loss of appetite, loss of sleep, loss of hope. Loss of libido is also a common symptom, but in our neuterized atmosphere it can also be seen as a cause of depression. As one researcher put it, "Enforced abstinence may be a precipitating factor."

"There is the big and the little solitude," said Danielle, the divorced mother of a fifteen-year-old girl. "The big solitude is a hole that cannot be filled. I no longer try to fill it. The little solitude—the eating alone, the never going out—I try to do something about. I have to watch myself or I'd eat breakfast all day. I don't get dressed sometimes—I can't seem to get dressed just for myself."

The relationship between aging and depression is equivocal. Depression affects women at every age. A clear relationship between menopause and the onset of depression has never been demonstrated, yet menopause (or what it signifies) can exacerbate a preexisting depressive state. Some doctors think that the rapid drop of hormones that can accompany menopause may affect certain susceptible people. If estrogen is given to relieve depression in menopausal women, in certain instances it seems to work. But apart from the placebo effect, this may also be due to the fact that estrogen does clearly stop hot flashes and vaginal dryness. A woman who is sleeping better because she no longer suffers severe nocturnal hot flashes, or who feels more womanly because her vagina is better lubricated, may feel generally more cheerful. In most cases, however, estrogen does nothing to relieve depression, and may even exacerbate it.

But although depression can occur at any age, female suicide attempts peak between the ages of forty-five and fifty-four. Often these attempts are unsuccessful, and can be read as last-ditch cries for help. Elderly women who attempt suicide, however, generally succeed, as do men. Evidently the old in our society no longer feel even enough hope to hedge their bets when they attempt suicide.

The core of depression has been defined as a sense of loss of the future. If this is so, it is not difficult to see why so many postmenopausal women are depressed. We are not imagining the bleakness of our tomorrows; for many of us this is an altogether reasonable expectation. As I look at the faces and bodies of older women on buses, on streets, in stores, I get the impression that a pall of depression hovers over too many of us. Our styleless clothes, slouched bodies, tired gaits, and listless eyes arouse in me a tangle of empathy and repulsion, solidarity and anger. Empathy because I too know how it feels—from inside. Repulsion because I want to flee from all the poverty, unhappiness, and self-hate. Solidarity because I know these are sisters whose suffering is akin to my own. And anger at a world that does not even have the decency to see this as oppression, but instead considers depression the normal, if somewhat pitiful, condition for decent, older women.

Emotional Problems: Agoraphobia

Agoraphobia: anxiety when walking across open spaces and through empty streets. It also occurs in crowded places or situations where one has a commitment to remain, like a supermarket checkout line or a doctor's office. These situations evoke fear of being trapped, of attracting unwanted attention, of dying. Distance from home exaggerates the problem, and being with a supportive person often helps.

Agoraphobia, along with depression, epitomizes the condition of older women. When I think about it, I get visions of Socrates walking the agora with his students—all male and young—creating the basis for Western civilization. They are at home, on their turf, as men in patriarchal societies always feel as they occupy public spaces. Public space is male space. Women are there on sufferance—if not as interlopers, then as prey. Rape and street harassment carry with them the male territorial imperative, with its implicit message: you are on my territory and so you are fair game. Women in these situations feel agoraphobic— that is, "trapped, subject to unwanted attention, or dead (nonexistent)."

No wonder the Athenian women were in the house. From classical times, we have been socialized to be agoraphobics. There are at least two female agoraphobics to every male. Its onset is later than that of other phobias, generally not starting until the twenties—the time when women first assume the adult female role. It can persist indefinitely. Being away from secure surroundings is so threatening that the agoraphobic lives a severely restricted life, often unable even to run simple errands.

Agoraphobia is emblematic of the way women turn legitimate complaints against themselves. Most agoraphobics consider themselves incapable of assertive, independent actions. The psychiatrist Wolpe says that it often develops in women who had overprotective mothers and absent fathers. If we look at the symptom as a communication, it is as if the person is saying, "You will not let me do the independent things that I want to do. You have made me afraid to do them. But I dare not complain to you—I will instead exaggerate my incapacity and take it out on myself."

But agoraphobia is also an indirect form of revenge. It invariably affects other members of the family, since they have to take over the domestic and social responsibilities of the sufferer. And so the agoraphobic is also saying, "You never wanted to give me my fair share of the world. Well, now you can have it—but you will pay."

Like depression, agoraphobia is considered normal for women, especially older women. We are expected to like to stay home, to feel uncomfortable in public places without escorts. Thus, agoraphobia is not seen as particularly disabling if one is older and female. This common viewpoint is articulated in a medical text about the problem. The authors conclude that "if the patient is the wife, there is no good evidence for any substantial detrimental effect on family life, if we exclude those routines, such as shopping, that are directly affected by the patient's avoidance behavior." Evidently, a good wife and mother does not have to work, does not care to go to museums, movies, and meetings—or in other ways participate in the world at large. It's a relatively simple matter to take over her shopping. And if she is an older woman— well, even less need for her to leave the house! I am convinced that much agoraphobia goes undetected, so closely does it match people's idea of an appropriate life style for older women.

Treating "Women's Complaints"

When women blame themselves for their troubles, they are only echoing society's attitude. The medical profession must assume a major portion of the responsibility for that attitude. Rather than the real sources of distress for older women—the youth culture and the double standard of aging—the American way is to locate the source of the trouble in the individual woman and then treat her—usually with drugs or surgery.

Of course, relief of suffering should not be denied to anybody. But all too often women are given inappropriate treatment and their real complaints remain undiagnosed, trivialized, or dismissed.

We all too often concur in this approach. Every time a woman takes a pill instead of making needed changes in her circumstances, she is also swallowing the message "The problem lies within me." This kind of treatment exacerbates the very problems it tries to solve by reinforcing our tendency to see our complaints as personal rather than as social problems.

Our Doctors, Ourselves

Many male doctors subscribe to stereotypes about older women, which are unfortunately shared by many of their patients. We are all too willing to give our bodies over to the doctors, who are annoyed by us but who have a vested interest in our dependency.

Doctors find us irritating because we report too many symptoms. They are taught to look for clear-cut organic disease—never mind that these diseases come packaged in real people with complex needs! Men, who underreport symptoms, are taken more seriously by doctors, and are treated for organic illness (whether or not they have it). Male doctors identify with middle-aged men under pressure, but women are more often dismissed as having "psychosomatic" complaints.

"Females have more time to indulge in neurosis than men. They're bored and often frustrated. As they get older, there's the menopause, which we men do not indulge in," said one doctor. Researchers Michele Barrett and Helen Rogers found that doctors saw women's problems as originating in the home, rather than stemming from lack of opportunity. Working women under stress were counseled to give up their jobs. Doctors could not understand a woman's complaints because she had "a nice home, doting husband, and lovely kids." When asked to describe a "typical complaining patient," 72 percent of doctors in another study made her female.

We tend to agree that we are a nuisance. We are reluctant to criticize the doctor, usually accept his view that our ailments are not serious, and are concerned about "taking up his time."

Medical texts and articles which describe untreated menopause as a "dismal change" or a "deficiency disease" and call us "pitiful creatures" are still in use. And descriptions of sex and aging in professional literature are heavily loaded with descriptions of female changes in appearance:

> Women in their middle years present different body contours: skin elasticity decreases everywhere in the body, the breasts sag, the abdominal skin is often wrinkled and scarred with purple stretch marks, the muscles of the limbs show increasing lack of muscle tone, and the "battle" of various bulges may be under way.

There is no corresponding description of male changes in appearance. The following is my own:

> Men in their middle years present different body contours, hair loss is common, skin elasticity decreases everywhere in the body, a tendency to accumulate large fatty deposits over the abdomen is noticeable, skin wrinkles and discolors, and muscles of the limbs show a lack of tone and mass, resulting in the storklike appearance of many older men.

Hysterectomy

When I was in my thirties, my reputable Yale gynecologist told me that if I was *really* serious about birth control, I would have a hysterectomy, because the uterus had no function other than pregnancy. I was one of the 50 percent of all women patients so counseled. But in a longitudinal heart disease study done in Framingham, Massachusetts, it was found that women who had a simple hysterectomy (with ovaries remaining) ran a two to three times greater risk of coronary heart disease. Evidently, the uterus has a protective function. It also has a sexual function. Of the women who have had hysterectomies, 35 percent report less intense orgasm. In spite of medical pooh-poohing, this isn't a farfetched idea, since during orgasm the cervix, uterus, and ovaries can contract rhythmically—if they are there.

Hysterectomy is the most common operation performed in the United States and the most lucrative one that gynecologists do. The rate has started to decline slightly in recent years, but approximately one out of every four women still ends up having one.

The need for hysterectomy is extremely subjective. When indicated, it can be the treatment of choice, even a life-saving procedure. However, only 10 to 20 percent of all hysterectomies are done in response to life-threatening conditions, such as intractable infection, hemorrhage, or cancer. Studies show that many more hysterectomies are done under fee-for-service medical systems like ours than in countries with national health plans. It has also been shown that in the United States the number performed varies with the number of hospital beds available and with the patient's ability to pay.

Some women feel positive about their hysterectomies. "It was a blessed relief to get rid of the whole kit," said Carole. "Sex is better now, without worrying about conception, and I feel so much healthier." A retired prostitute told me that she had been trying to get one ever since she was eighteen and finally at thirty-five found a doctor who would do it. "I have no regrets," she added.

Others, like Chantal, reported painful feelings of anger, loss, and neutering. "It was a major blow to my self-esteem," she said. "Sex feels different now, and my stomach muscles have never been the same." All operations are, of course, emotionally traumatic. But there are about three times as many psychiatric referrals after hysterectomies than after operations not connected to the sexual-reproductive organs.

Women and Drugs: Estrogen

We are expected to have a difficult time in midlife, and much of this is blamed on "the change." Medical schools still teach that there is something called "postmenopausal syndrome," a mythical clinical entity consisting of everything that might ail an older woman, including headaches, irritability, depression, insomnia, hot flashes, joint and muscle aches, tiredness, and vaginal dryness. Out of this grab bag, the only symptoms that are clearly due to estrogen reduction are vaginal dryness and hot flashes. They respond promptly to estrogen replacement therapy, although its use even in these instances is controversial. Estrogen is generally not indicated for the other symptoms, and may even exacerbate some of them. Yet over $70 million worth of Premarin is sold annually, enough to supply 5 million women, although only about 1.5 million women are menopausal each year—and most of them are not significantly incapacitated either by hot flashes or vaginal dryness.

Substance Abuse

Where older women and drugs are concerned, estrogen replacement is just the beginning. The double standard of aging extends to other drug treatment. About 70 percent of psychoactive drugs, such as tranquilizers, barbiturates, antidepressants, and amphetamines, are prescribed to women, and the largest single group taking these drugs is middle-aged women. Valium is the most prescribed drug in the country, with women the major users. Ninety percent of emergency room overdoses in one study involved women, with middle-aged white women overrepresented. Tranquilizers rank with heroin as the major cause of overdose emergencies.

Some of the blame for this situation must be laid at the door of the drug companies themselves, which spend over $4,200 per physician per year to promote sales. Researchers Prather and Fiddell did a content analysis of drug advertisements in leading medical journals over a five-year period and came to the following conclusions:

(1) The sex stereotypes were confirmed virtually without exception in the advertisements.
(2) There was a strong tendency to associate psychoactive drugs with female patients (although not out of proportion to the prescription rates for women).
(3) Nonpsychoactive drug advertisements usually showed a male as the patient, despite the fact that women also take more nonpsychoactive drugs than do men. (I find this difference particularly insidious because it indicates that men have "real" illnesses while women show mental problems.)
(4) The symptoms listed for male and female users of psychoactive drugs were significantly different, with men usually presenting specific and work-related symptoms while women complained of diffuse anxiety, tension, and depression.
(5) Male patients were shown at a wider variety of ages than female patients.
(6) There was a tendency to show women as recuperating from mental illness when they reassumed sex-stereotypical attitudes, as irritating significant others by their illness, and as suffering from socially embarrassing symptoms.

Women's drug use appears legitimate because it is largely prescribed, while men tend to use more nonlegal drugs like heroin and cocaine. But legal addiction is still addiction. Doctors are more willing to give tranquilizers to a "housewife who can always take a nap and need not be mentally alert." Eighty-seven percent of physicians in another study thought that Librium was fine for homemakers but not for students.

To this picture of widespread drug abuse add several different drugs taken together, then also add alcohol and mix well. This pattern of mixed drug and alcohol dependency is all too common. Almost half of women drug takers use at least two; Dr. Sadja Greenwood, a women's physician in San Francisco, calls drug interactions a "hazard of aging in this overmedicated society."

Today there are as many female as male alcoholics, with the mean age in the middle to late forties. A Menninger Clinic study showed that the largest proportion of women began serious drinking to cope with the death or departure of husband and/or children. They went downhill so rapidly that the course of their drinking is described as "attenuated suicide."

Substance Abuse: Food

Mary, a fifty-five-year-old mother of six, considers herself to be about twenty-five pounds overweight. "Every year I gain about five pounds, and every year it gets harder and harder to take them off," she says. "When I go on a diet my husband and children complain that I don't make the gravies and desserts they like. 'We are not on diets,' they tell me. I give up," she adds with a laugh. "I guess it's just a matter of age."

Women gain weight at the same time that they lose their youth. On the average, there is a sixteen-pound jump from the twenties to the fifties. For men the comparable increase is only six pounds.

The cause of this, however, is not what Mary thinks. Age does not automatically add pounds, nor do the hormonal changes of menopause. Weight gain after youth is caused, as at any other age, by eating more than one needs. We simply need less food as we get older, particularly if we become less active. But we often don't adjust our appetites to our changing physical needs, for several reasons.

In the first place, it is hard to cut back on the gratifications of eating at a time when other gratifications are falling away. Giselle, a woman in her fifties, put it this way: "I torture myself going on diets, and what is the point? Whether I'm fat or skinny, it makes no difference. I look after my mother, I go to work. Why go to all the trouble when at least I can have the enjoyment of eating."

Gaining weight if you are an older woman has certain meanings and consequences in our culture. There *are* cultures where it carries sexual and/or social prestige, but ours is not one of them. In the classic patriarchies of southern Europe, older women become imposing figures by reasons of their girth, and wield a corresponding household power. But in white America, fatness is largely penalized. This is unfair to women for whom generous proportions are a natural and desirable state. For the rest of us, getting fat is gratuitously self-destructive.

Although it may also have some payoffs, weight gain is a classic "women's complaint." Susie Orbach, in her book *Fat Is a Feminist Issue*, talks about the multiple meanings of female fat—such as rebellion, protection, assertion, denial, punishment. Gaining weight in our later years may have all these meanings—and others besides.

We get fat because we give up. "My fat is my despair," said Priscilla. We "let ourselves go." Where? To seed, to pasture, to the dogs. Finally the endless struggle to Look Good For Them no longer pays off, and we drop the project—perhaps with relief and even defiance.

It's fine to stop trying to please Them. But when we gain too much weight, we lose for ourselves the payoff of being in optimum physical condition. Like other symptoms of maladaptive aging, it is a way of taking out our malaise on ourselves. It completes our alienation from our bodies.

Adding pounds is a symptom of our surrender to the neutering process. Because fat is considered unattractive in our culture, being overweight reveals our own lack of esteem for our bodies. In "letting ourselves go" we let go of our hopes for being powerful, sexual, socially desirable human beings. We join a caste of second-class citizens called "matrons," for which the passport is a "matronly" figure. But who can blame us?

Our culture tells us that this is the inevitable fate for midlife women—with the exception of movie star types and "beautiful people." And so we don't have to feel guilty anymore about not measuring up. Society is ready for us with a comfy pigeonhole. There are dowdy styles and half sizes, elastic stockings and orthopedic shoes, even the women's movement and the older women's movement. And once we get kicked up onto this rung of the ladder, not too much is expected—or demanded—of us.

We can give ourselves the middle-aged makeover and relax into matronhood.

Matrons

Webster's tells us that the word "matron" derives from Latin and means "a married woman usually marked by dignified maturity or social distinction." But for modern matrons the substance of this definition is gone. What remains are the taboos against "undignified" behavior—without the corresponding clout.

However, not all women that our culture labels "matrons" accept such a confining definition of themselves. There are those who feel positive about themselves and their bodies. Some of them are matrons in the older, Latin sense—women who have carved out a sphere of influence and distinction, like Paula, a black social worker who comes from a ghetto background. "In my family," she says, "women were powerful, and all of us were big. I cannot conceive of losing weight without losing power." And then there is Helen, a natural contemplative for whom her solitude is a blessing. "I have had some out-of-the-body experiences where I floated up to the ceiling and looked down on myself," she said. "When I saw my body I thought, 'I like my body. It's like a pillow.'"

And there is Mary, who raised three children with her optometrist husband before moving to San Francisco and getting involved in the older women's lesbian community. "We started a group called Fat, Female, and Forty," she laughs. "It did great things for me. Even before I was fat, while I was living with my husband, I never liked my body. Now I accept it—although I would not say I feel great about the way I eat through my stress. But this business of always having to look a certain way to be loved is ridiculous. None of my friends look like models, but to cuddle up to a woman who has some meat on her feels wonderful."

These women and others like them have bucked the mainstream and found ways outside it to affirm their bodies. For most of us, however, the matronly norm carries with it a lower level of prestige and well-being. A subtle process takes place whereby we cash in our positive image of ourselves after youth in response to minor physical changes. If we feel a bit out of shape or overweight, we may moan but we don't take care of it the way we might have at thirty. We blame it on getting older, not on the true culprits: negative images of aging or lack of reason to stay fit. The more we have to live for, the more reason we have to take care of ourselves.

"After fifty," says Dr. Greenwood, "the influence of body image and life style is crucial. Women who are resigned to becoming limited, women who eat, smoke or drink to excess, age very differently from women who don't."

For the first time in history, it is now possible to feel and look vital and remain active for all of our lives. This possibility is due not to a new wonder drug, but to a new understanding of our choices.

For older women to actively choose well-being has revolutionary implications, because it means that we stop turning our complaints against ourselves and that we do something about them. Without this outer focus, it is impossible to heal ourselves. And, conversely, if we are going to do something about our "complaints," we will need all the help we can get from our well-loved, well-cared-for bodies.

9

RE-OWNING OUR BODIES

If I had only known what I was doing to myself! If I had only under-stood twenty years ago the futility, the alienation, the self-denigration of trying to fit oneself into a mold. It was as if I was thinking of myself as a product rather than a person. I had yet to learn that the most in-credible beauty and the most satisfying way of life come from affirming your own uniqueness, making the most of what you really are. The glow and energy of the healthy woman is the ultimate beauty, the only beauty that will last.

Jane Fonda's Workout Book

Image Changing

And so we begin to dare to say it—not only with our words but also with our bodies. Don't count us out because we are over forty. We are still in the running, sexually, socially, and vocation-ally. We will not cooperate in making ourselves over into the neg-ative image you have of us. We reserve the right to age. But we also claim our right to look well and feel well—better than any of us would have dreamed twenty years ago.

We now know that the body is marvelously adaptable in hith-erto unsuspected ways. As therapist Don Johnson writes:

In the foot, for example, the 28 bones and 32 joints provide only a very general outline for an eventual shape. The curve of its potential arches, the organization of the toes, the position of the heel in relation to the lower leg are all to be determined. Even for an adult, there are numerous possibilities for change. We might, for example, feed into a computer the structural variations available to a particular 45-year-old woman, along with all the conceivable methods she might use during the next ten years to realize one possibility or another. One track might include daily yoga, therapeutic massage and golf. Another might involve months in bed with a serious illness. Another might involve her encountering a new and exciting lover. Examining the results of all conceivable programs, we would find a wide range of possible relationships among her head, chest, pelvis and feet.

People usually think their bodies are largely the inevitable product of forces beyond their control. This is not the case. Our bodies are records of our lives as we have lived them up to now. They record not only inevitabilities, but also choices. They can change as our lives change, and respond to change in our beliefs and attitudes.

Our feelings about ourselves affect our posture, breathing, and muscle tone. Even our hormone levels have been shown to be responsive to our thoughts. For example, if we think we are over the hill, we may be inhibiting the production of the female hormones estrogen and progesterone. Our beliefs about aging can affect our very cells.

Conversely, the actual state of our bodies holds and grounds our body images. For example, it is harder to feel sprightly and energetic with a compressed spine. Changes in our bodies powerfully affect our sense of who we are.

We don't even know what aging would look like in a society that was supportive of it. In a culture where women were part of the mainstream for their entire life span, we would surely age differently. We can see this beginning to happen as a significant minority of fortunate older women begin to change their attitude toward aging.

The first step, as we decide to undertake this journey, is to be compassionate with ourselves. Whatever we are today, we can understand how we got here without beating ourselves for it. We declare a truce with our bodies, and begin a new relationship with them. As we start to listen to them, we are awed by the way they have helped us. Many of our "symptoms" or "complaints" have been bodily strategies for helping us survive painful situations. Of course, we show signs of wear and tear, but we have earned them—wrinkles, sags, bulges, or whatever.

We also accept our cyclic physiology, not as a nuisance to be tolerated, but as a positive aspect of our natures. We accept menopause as an opportunity to experience a profound physiological change that men cannot experience, and that opens up to us opportunities for new sensibilities.

Accepting ourselves does *not* mean being resigned to unnecessary disabilities. "The women of my village are old at forty," says a character in a film by Bernard Tavernier, *A Week's Vacation.* "They are not old physically, but one day they sit on a bench and bury their youth." We do not have to run backward toward youth, but neither do we have to sit on a park bench and bury it.

My friend Leona Bayer is a (mostly) retired pediatrician of eighty. She still goes for a morning swim in San Francisco Bay and carries a full schedule of speaking engagements and community activities. She is about to leave on a trip for China. Leona is much in demand for interviews and studies about optimal aging. "Aging is getting to be a new profession," she laughs. When I admired the way she braves the cold waters of the bay, she responded, "Well, my husband and I always enjoyed it and I see no reason to stop. It sure kills the whole morning, though." Then she added, "I hurt my hip a few months ago, but it's better now. You know, when you are young and you hurt something, you assume it will get better. When you are older, sometimes you think it will never get better, but it will. It's important to know that, and to keep being as active as you can."

We must reassert our final authority over our own bodies. We know more about what we need than anybody else, since no two bodies are alike, and they are *our* bodies, aren't they? This doesn't mean discarding expert opinion where relevant. It does mean learning to be aware of what our bodies are telling us they *really* need. In this way, we can guide ourselves toward the changes and decisions that are appropriate for each of us. Learning to listen to that "still, small voice" takes practice, but it is a skill, like any other, that develops with practice.

Eating

One woman who started listening to the still, small voice described the change in her eating habits that then took place:

The illusion that food will fill me no longer works. It doesn't have the same taste. As I define and differentiate myself, the clearer my shape becomes. My body takes on a more defined look; it's more at my command. My repertoire of understanding what I need is much larger. If it's a need to be comforted, I have to find a way to be comforted—not just eat. And if I can't do this, I can tolerate the pain better. I'd rather get into bed, turn on the electric blanket and cry than deal with neurotic pain. The experience of dealing with the feeling itself rather than not dealing with it feels so much better! One learns how to go into the abyss and not wallow in it but come out and keep on with life.

Underneath the screams of the old habits has the still, small voice also been telling you to change your eating? Are there days when you simply are not hungry, or when you want less meat or protein in general? Or plainer, less rich food?

With recent nutritional research, now widely available, we know that the American diet is too high in salt, fat, meat, and refined carbohydrates like white flour and sugar, too low in fiber from unrefined grains and vegetables. These facts have special implications for older women. Epidemiological studies of Japanese women show that breast cancer is correlated with high-fat diets. Some of these women moved to the United States and their diets became more Westernized; their rate of breast cancer increased proportionately. High-fat diets also increase constipation, and it is thought that this in turn causes estrogen to recirculate in the body. Increased levels of this hormone are associated with breast cancer.

Another diet-related problem for older women is osteoporosis, the "little old lady" syndrome. As we get older, our calcium metabolism can become less efficient, with resulting demineralization of the skeletal structure. The bones become porous and fragile, particularly the weight-bearing bones of the spine and hip. White, small-boned, thin women are particularly susceptible.

Osteoporosis is aggravated by high-protein diets. As we age, our need for protein decreases. All we need is about 50 grams per day, but the average American meat-eater gets twice this amount. Excess protein creates a chemical condition which causes calcium to be excreted in the urine. Diets high in meat are also implicated in cancer of the colon, which is, after breast cancer, the most common cause of cancer death in women.

The use of estrogen to treat osteoporosis is controversial, but it appears that improvement does occur for a limited time—about three years. However, dietary calcium supplementation and decrease of excess protein are indefinitely effective, particularly in conjunction with exercise.

Use It or Lose It

Exercise is an essential component in any regime of self-care. Vigorous activity prevents osteoporosis by stimulating the bones to lay down more calcium. The value of aerobics (the kind of exercise that makes you sweat and pant) for everything from appetite regulation to the prevention of heart disease to the treatment of depression has been widely disseminated.

As we get older, we need to do what I call anti-gravity exercises, in addition to aerobics. Over the years, the constant downward pull of gravity on our faces and bodies compresses us and causes sagging, tension, and malfunction of our joints and internal organs. The tone and elasticity of the muscular system can be maintained by gentle, sensual stretching. Note that the face is part of the body! It too can be kept in tone. This benefits appearance, and also releases emotional tension from the facial muscles. These muscles of expression store a great deal of tension, which can cause fatigue, depression, and headaches. Even vision can be affected. A modest program of selective stretching can maintain expressiveness, balance, and flexibility indefinitely.

Older women should also know about Kegel exercises. Originally developed by the doctor of the same name to combat urinary incontinence, they can be an important component of a sexual self-care program as well. These exercises use the pubococcygeous muscle, which runs from the pubic bone in front to the coccyx at the end of the spine. In it are the three body openings. When you sit on the toilet and stop the flow of urine, you are using the pubococcygeous, or PC. Women can learn to alternately contract and release this muscle, which keeps it in tone. This tightens the vagina and improves urinary continence, and will also intensify orgasm (or bring it about in preorgasmic women). Kegel exercises can be done (secretly) anywhere.

Exercise is about play, about fun, about self-love. It need not be a grim duty, nor a task that absorbs huge amounts of time. It is a great way of re-owning one's body.

Sexuality and Sensuality

"I hope I never lose my lust," said Mara, an editor at a small publishing house. Many of the powerful women I met acknowledged the connection between sexuality and life energy. We can counteract the neutering atmosphere of our society by consciously exercising our sexual "muscles." Some of these are literally muscles, and some are muscles of the imagination.

The best cure for vaginal atrophy is an active sex life—alone, or with a partner, or both. Learning how to enjoy your own body is an important part of knowing how to love and appreciate yourself. This can become increasingly important as we get older, whether we have lovers or not. Masturbation is a natural Kegel exercise. It also can tone the muscles of the abdomen, buttocks, and legs. The sensations can be intensified with erotic fantasy and the use of aids like vibrators or dildoes. It is an excellent form of relaxation and stress release, which are important components of self-care. Skillful masturbation can be learned; Lonnie Barbach's book, *For Yourself*, is an excellent guide.

Keeping the juices flowing can take other forms as well, if we remain open-minded. Sometimes younger men are appreciative of our charms when our peers are not. And a number of women who have led heterosexual lives turn to other women for intimacy, support, and physical love. Samantha, who has three grandchildren, said, "After all, why not? The guys just aren't around, and even when they are, women are so much easier to talk to, to relate to. By this age my identity is centered in myself and it is not threatened by having a partner of the same sex. The women's community is marvelous, and I have better sex now than I ever had before, with women who are not hung up on the youth and appearance trip."

In their later years, many sexually active women seem to be more interested in pleasing themselves than in pleasing others. As women age and opportunities for sexual experience decline, so do opportunities for other forms of touch. And yet the emotional importance of tactile stimulation cannot be overestimated. As the psychologist Alexander Lowen says, "An ego that is not grounded in the reality of bodily feeling becomes desperate." The most intense form of touch is, perhaps, sexual penetration, but even a glance can be said to be penetrating when it truly connects. Sight and hearing are also surrogates of touch, but contact through these senses as well can be sharply reduced as women age. We often are forced to live in an atmosphere of sensory deprivation, which amounts to emotional starvation and ego murder. This is an insulting situation, in the sense of the word "insult" as a physical wound. As Ashley Montagu writes: "One has only to observe the responses of older people to a caress, an embrace, a handpat or clasp, to appreciate how vitally necessary such experiences are for their well-being. . . . Many an illness . . . has been greatly influenced by the quality of tactile support the individual has received before and during the illness."

We all need "strokes." "Tactless" people "rub us the wrong way." One wonders how many visits to doctors and beauty salons are indirect ways of getting back "in touch." Many older women also take great pleasure in pets for this reason. We need to create a climate in which touching, sexually or otherwise, is an accepted part of life for everyone. It is *not* acceptable for older women to go through life as the "untouchables" of society.

Menopause

Menopause has finally begun to be seen as a natural process and not a disease or a catastrophe. Yet most literature on menopause lines up with the male anti-body ethic, taking the position that women should get through it with as little fuss as possible. "Not to be bothered" is seen as the best possible outcome.

Most women give at least lip service to this position. Making a big deal out of menopause seems to have gone out of style with the Victorians. But I wonder if we are cheating ourselves. Why do we not choose to mark menopause with a rite of passage (apart from surgery!) as we mark our other transitions? Perhaps because in our society the top rung of the ladder is not braced against anything solid. When we reach it, we tend to find ourselves jumping off into midair.

But a few exceptional women *are* making a fuss about menopause—in a new spirit. A therapist who works in the tradition of Wilhelm Reich described her passage to me in her thoughtful, serene voice:

My menopause coincided with the collapse of my marriage, and I went through a period of real collapse. I decided to let myself fully experience the fear that other people tranquilize, and it was rough. I couldn't even walk up the street—just spiraled around in bed with acute attacks of vertigo. But I refused to quit; something inside me wanted to experience being really alone. My fear felt connected to an old fear of coming out of the womb—a fear of not being contained or held. The hot flashes were very frightening at first. I felt real panic.

What is so frightening about all this is that the body begins to take over, and we are so unused to this that we interfere with its progress. But if you can allow that—the body does heal itself. I had done a good deal of bioenergetic therapy [a form of Reichian body therapy] and I connected the flashes with those feelings of energy rushing through me. I still get them, but I know now how to ground them—to send the energy down into my legs. They now move up and down and it's OK—I am using the new energy. It's the sudden ungrounded upflow in women who are not used to letting go of this energy that takes them off their feet and is so scary.

I quite like my hot flashes now. If you just relax and let them happen they can be quite enjoyable.

The theme of spiritual opening was discussed by the psychologist Edith Sullwold. "Rituals should happen naturally," she told me. "When a young girl starts to menstruate, she should be given a bouquet of red roses. And when I went through menopause, my clients started to give me violets—the color of spirituality."

In an inspired article in *Co-Evolution Quarterly* called the "Space Crone," Ursula LeGuin talks about capitalizing on the two biological transitions in our lives (menarche, menopause). She sees the "change of life" as an opportunity to become a Crone:

The woman who is willing to make that change must become pregnant with herself, at last. She must bear herself, her third self, her old age, with travail and alone. That pregnancy is long, that labor is hard. Only one is harder, and that's the final one, the one which men also must suffer and perform.

It may well be easier to die if you have already given birth to others or yourself, at least once before. This would be an argument for going through all the discomfort and embarrassment of becoming a Crone. Anyhow it seems a pity to have a built-in rite of passage and to dodge it, to evade it, and pretend nothing has changed. That is to dodge and evade one's womanhood, to pretend one's like a man. Men, once initiated, never get the second chance. They never change again. That's their loss, not ours. Why borrow poverty?

Certainly the effort to remain unchanged, young, when the body gives so impressive a signal of change as the menopause, is gallant; but it is a stupid, self-sacrificial gallantry, better befitting a boy of twenty than a woman of forty-five or fifty. Let the athletes die young and laurel-crowned. Let the soldiers earn the Purple Hearts. Let women die old, white-crowned, with human hearts.

By affirming the importance of menopause, we validate the second half of our lives. The top rung of the ladder does lead somewhere—and women such as these are exploring this new territory. It is likely that many problems now associated with menopause would be alleviated if such an attitude were more prevalent.

Support: Overcoming Agoraphobia

When we turn our complaints outward instead of inward, we find each other. Instead of internalizing our problems, remaining isolated, and getting our symptoms treated, we can help each other to come out of the closet and out of the house.

"There is a crying need for menopause support groups, and for education about optimal aging," says Dr. Greenwood. "Women who understand these processes seem to be much less upset about them. And men need to understand what menopause and aging are about, too."

Our lifelong conditioning to agoraphobic modes of behavior makes support a necessary precondition for change. But even with it, change may not come easy.

Once we turn our complaints outward, we target their real source. This, in effect, makes demands on others to change. We then risk the usual reprisals directed at older women, ridicule and hostility. But, at the very least, we will be invisible no more.

The choice is ours to make. Re-owning our bodies will not make all life's problems go away, but it can make them seem less like obstacles and more like challenges. Besides, being in shape is both a sign of and a precondition for power. It will help us to take on the sobering and exhilarating challenges that lie ahead.

The suggestions of doctors Greenwood and Margolis that follow are a helpful guide toward owning our own bodies.

Suggestions for Nutrition, Exercise, and Relaxation for Older Women

SADJA GREENWOOD, M.D.
ALAN J. MARGOLIS, M.D.

You can feel vital and energetic in middle age and after if you pay attention to what you eat and how you live. Also, you can reduce your chances of getting heart disease, high blood pressure, various cancers, diabetes, brittle bones, and many other illnesses. Here are some simple suggestions for nutrition, exercise, and relaxation which can be of help.

NUTRITION

Vegetables, whole grains, fruits should be staples in your diet. They provide most of the needed nutrients, and lots of fiber for combating constipation. Eat fresh food of many types when it is in season. Unsprayed produce is best if available. Emphasize deep green and yellow vegetables for vitamins and minerals. Potatoes and sweet potatoes are very healthy foods. All members of the bean family (fresh and dried beans, peas, lentils, bean sprouts, and tofu) have generous amounts of protein. Eat whole grains—whole wheat, rye, oats, barley, corn, and brown rice. Tofu, tempeh,* or beans with a whole grain make a complete protein comparable to meat.

DON'T EAT *White bread, sweet rolls, cakes, white spaghetti— use whole grains.*

Canned vegetables—too much salt—use fresh.

Canned fruit—too much sugar—use fresh.

* Soybean products of Oriental origin—available in Oriental or health food stores.

Meat, poultry, and fish. We should eat less meat, poultry, and fish as we age for two main reasons. They are often high in fat, which may promote heart disease. Their high protein content is processed by the body in a way that promotes loss of calcium from the bones (women who do not take estrogens after the menopause should get most of their protein from beans, whole grains, vegetables, and low-fat milk products, and use meat very little).

DON'T EAT *Bacon, ham, lunch meat, pressed and processed meats—they are too high in salt, fat and chemicals.*

The skin on poultry, the fat around meat, gravy.

Milk, yogurt, cheese. Non-fat and low-fat milk, yogurt, and cottage cheese are good foods in menopause because of their calcium content. Also high in calcium: corn tortillas, sesame and sunflower seeds, soybeans, tofu, broccoli, collards, kale, and mustard greens.

DON'T EAT *Cream, sour cream, ice cream—too much fat.*

CAUTION *Butter—high in fat, use very sparingly.*

Hard cheeses—high in fat and salt, use sparingly.

Eggs are a good protein food but are high in fat and cholesterol, which can promote heart disease. It is prudent to limit yourself to three or four eggs a week in middle age. Know your serum cholesterol and keep it below 200.

DON'T EAT *Fried eggs, cheese omelets, etc.—too much fat.*

Egg substitutes—too many chemicals.

Fats such as butter, margarine, oil, mayonnaise, cream, and lard are very high in calories but contain few nutrients. They can contribute to obesity and heart disease and should be used *very* sparingly in your daily diet.

CAUTION *avocado, seeds, nuts, and nut butters are nutritious foods but very high in fats—don't overdo.*

Sugar, as in table sugar, cakes, cookies, ice cream, candy, soft drinks, many packaged foods, and cold cereals, promotes tooth decay and tooth loss, and gives calories without nutrients. Sugar should be avoided for optimum health. When you crave something sweet, try a dried fig, a date, or a tangerine. You will be able to re-educate your taste buds!

DON'T USE *saccharine or diet drinks—too many chemicals.*

CAUTION *honey, maple sugar, and molasses contain more nutrients than white sugar, but should be used very sparingly.*

DO *clear sugary foods out of your kitchen and get a supply of fruit for your cravings.*

Salt (sodium) is a major contributor to high blood pressure and should be *greatly decreased* for optimum health. If your blood pressure is already high, eliminate salt completely. At the same time, increase your potassium intake by eating more fruits and vegetables.

CAUTION *canned soup, canned vegetables, pickles, packaged foods, restaurant food, soy sauce, tamari, miso contain too much salt.*

DO *use onions, garlic, lemons, and herbs/spices to flavor your food.*

Alcohol. If you want to drink, do so only in small quantities. Alcohol gives calories without nutrients, and is addicting to many people. It may make hot flushes more pronounced. Enjoy it occasionally in small amounts!

DON'T DRINK *hard liquor—it is too strong.*

DON'T DRINK AT ALL *if you have an alcohol problem—go to AA instead.*

DON'T DRINK *if it gives you heart palpitations or makes you dizzy or hung over. Your body can't recuperate as easily in middle age.*

Caffeine in coffee, tea (black and green), colas, and chocolate should be eliminated by most people. Caffeine creates anxiety and insomnia, and it contributes to breast lumps in women. It may make hot flashes more pronounced. Coffee has been associated with cancer of the pancreas. If you drink decaffeinated coffee, use the water-extracted beans. Try drinking herbal teas and cereal "coffees" instead, such as Cafix or Postum.

Nutritional supplements. The role of vitamin and mineral supplements in promoting health and alleviating symptoms is controversial, but we will make some suggestions based on current findings related to the menopause and middle age.

Calcium: Women in the menopause and beyond (especially those who choose not to take estrogens) are at risk for thinning of the bones (osteoporosis) and bone fractures. Supplemental calcium, along with Vitamin D to enhance absorption of calcium, will help to retard bone loss. We suggest one gram (1000 milligrams) daily of supplemental calcium and 400 IU Vitamin D daily (no more—Vitamin D can be toxic in high doses).

Multivitamins and Trace Minerals: A vitamin/mineral tablet supplying approximately the RDA (Recommended Daily Allowance) of all essential vitamins and minerals can act as an insurance that your nutrition is optimum every day.

Vitamin E: This vitamin has been suggested as helpful for many menopausal symptoms, including hot flushes and vaginal soreness. Many women take up to 400 IU daily. We are not aware of adverse effects of such large doses, but we feel that there has not been enough study of megavitamin therapy for us to endorse it completely.

DO EAT *a varied, nutritious diet including many vegetables, whole grains, and fruits, in order to get as many vitamins and minerals as possible from your food.*

DO SPEND *your money on food first rather than vitamins if money is short.*

DON'T *take too much of the fat-soluble vitamins, Vitamins A and D. They can be toxic in high doses:*
Vitamin D. Take 400 IU daily—not more.
Vitamin A. Do not take more than 5,000 units daily in a pill or capsule. Eat deep green vegetables, and yellow vegetables and fruits.

SMOKING

You are aware that smoking increases your risk of developing cancer of the lung and other sites (mouth, larynx, kidneys, bladder), emphysema, and heart attack. You may not know that smoking may affect how you look in middle age, by giving you more wrinkles! In addition, women smokers have an earlier and more problematic menopause, and are at greater risk of osteoporosis (brittle bones).

If you smoke, NOW is the time to quit.

EXERCISE

Exercise is vitally important to promote health and energy, and to keep your weight and "appestat" in balance. Since it is not a natural part of most city dwellers' lives, it must be consciously planned every day. Although it may seem hard to start exercising, you will quickly notice that it gives you more energy and relieves depression. Exercise is also essential to prevent osteoporosis, or thinning of the bones, as you age.

"Aerobic" exercise stimulates the heart and lungs and increases the oxygen used by the body. Examples are 20 minutes or more per day of brisk walking, dance, "jazzercise," swimming, bicycling, use of a stationary bicycle, or jogging. If you are over 40, inactive, and/or have a family or personal history of heart disease, you should start a walking program (work up from one mile to three-plus miles daily) and check with your doctor about safe ways to extend this if desired.

Flexibility and stretching exercises are important for the prevention of injury, for joint mobility, posture, and grace. Yoga, dance, calisthenics, and Tai Chi are examples.

Both kinds of exercise should be built into daily life in a way that is enjoyable to you. Once you begin a program of exercise that you enjoy, it can become a "positive addiction."

RELAXATION

When worries and pressures get overwhelming, many people try to find relief with medicines, drugs, or alcohol. However, there are natural ways to relax that will relieve tension and prevent or alleviate many illnesses. Some of these are meditation, yoga, biofeedback, prayer, massage, and music. Relaxation techniques will help you get through the menopause with more ease and balance.

References

Here are some paperback books you may find useful on the menopause, nutrition, exercise, and relaxation:

The Menopause: A Positive Approach, by Rosetta Reitz, Penguin, 1977.
The Emerging Woman: A Decade of Midlife Transitions, by Natalie Rogers, Personal Press, Box 789, Point Reyes Station, Calif. 94956.
The Menopause Book, ed. by Louisa Rose, E. P. Dutton, 1980.
Women, Menopause, and Middle Age, by Vidal Clay, Know, Inc., Pittsburgh, 1977.
Laurel's Kitchen, by Laurel Robertson, Carol Flinders, and Bronwen Godfrey, Nilgiri Press, 1976.
Nutrition Against Disease, by Roger Williams, Bantam, 1973.
The Wonderful World Within You: Your Inner Nutritional Environment, by Roger Williams, Bantam, 1977.
The Pritikin Program for Diet and Exercise, by Nathan Pritikin, Grosset & Dunlap, 1979.
The Aerobics Way, by Kenneth H. Cooper, J. Evans & Co., 1977.
Richard Hittleman's Yoga: 28 Day Exercise Plan, by Richard Hittleman, Bantam.
The Relaxation Response, by Herbert Benson, Avon Books, 1975.
90 Days to Self Health, by C. Norman Shealy, Dial Press, 1977.
The Relaxation and Stress Reduction Workbook, by Martha Davis, Matthew McKay, and Elizabeth Robbins Eshelman, New Harbinger Publications, 624 43rd Street, Richmond, Calif. 94805, 1980.

10

AUTHENTICITY

*Once upon a time a beautiful young woman stood weeping by the edge
of a pond. As a handsome knight rode by, she fell on her knees, plead-
ing, "Oh, kind sir, I am the victim of a terrible sorcery. Only your kiss
can rescue me from my cruel fate." The knight dismounted with gallant alacrity and embraced the fair damsel and kissed her. Before his
eyes, she was transformed into a horny, wrinkled toad and with a croak
of thanks, she hopped into the pond.*

Exploring the Dark Side of the Moon

"I know who I am with my husband and kids," said Michelle, a
forty-five-year-old woman. "But who am I with me?"

Instead of pimples, it's hot flashes, but the questions "Who am
I?" and "What do I want to do?" are familiar. I heard them again
and again—and sometimes from women who seemed surprised
by their introspection. The dark side of the moon calls out for ex-
ploration; it is a summons to wholeness that can no longer be ignored. As the psychologist Abraham Maslow says, "A damaged
organism isn't content to be what it is . . . it fights and struggles to
make itself into a unity again."

When we talk about this urgent need to find out what else we
are besides Jimmy's mother and Harry's wife we are talking about
the mysterious and wonderful human journey toward personal authenticity.

The word "authentic" comes from the Greek *authentikos*, meaning to master, to accomplish. This implies activity. We do not so much "find" ourselves as accomplish ourselves. This takes work. But to older women, the need to undertake this work can feel as powerful as the need to breathe. Our finiteness presses down upon us.

"When you've got something inside that's not getting out, it depresses you," said Jane, an Englishwoman. "I've just gotten to the point where I'm playing with a full deck. Then you suddenly realize you might go out and get run over tomorrow—there's a panic about time. It would be extremely annoying to have that opportunity taken away, even though I'm still not sure what to do with it."

Sometimes the summons to authenticity is triggered by an incident:

I got pregnant—unexpectedly—at forty-five, after having tried for years to have another child and then just giving up. I was devastated, torn apart. I wanted the child, but I knew that if I went ahead with the pregnancy, *this was it*—eighteen more years of child care—no time ever, *ever* again to find out what else I was all about. It was agonizing, but I decided to risk my husband's disapproval, even him leaving me, and I had an abortion.

After I was told at fifty-eight that I had breast cancer and had three years to live, I decided that if I really had that long I could do anything. I just decided to quit stopping myself.

I looked at some pictures of a friend's son's bar mitzvah, and I couldn't find myself. "Where's the picture of me?" I asked. "You passed it, dummy," said my friend. And then I saw she was right. I hadn't recognized myself, because I never pictured myself as a fat, middle-aged matron. I decided there and then that it was *not* me. After being on a million diets, being addicted to pills, everything, I finally lost weight.

For others, it is a gradual awakening:

I saw my husband wasn't happy. I wanted to be the source of his joy and excitement, but it wasn't working. Finally I got tired of being a surrogate everything, and I turned my attention to me. The discovery of myself is incredible, and it's still going on.

The change at around forty for me was hard—it had something to do with getting back to who I was originally before reproduction. I can feel that now I would like to finally expand into being who I am, with no cosmetic restrictions.

And we need to finally come to terms with who we are not:

At some point you set aside the excuses and look at the truth. The truth was it was too late for me to be an artist. I probably didn't ever have the drive or talent to be first rate. That was a good thing to know. I'm a great appreciator, and I don't feel badly about it.

For women the desire to live authentically is still considered a bit peculiar, like wanting to be a wrestler or a telephone lineman. We don't quite have the hang of it yet. We sense that we are once again venturing out into male territory—a domain already defined by male psychologists and philosophers.

The usual stereotypes come to mind. Why should women worry about authenticity? Women are innately authentic, aren't they? They can't help it, they are so close to nature, and so forth. Or: women are intrinsically devious, duplicity is part of their nature—and even their charm. Where would we be without our "feminine wiles"?

The truth is that authenticity up until now has been a luxury that women have not been able to afford. Our dependence on men has taught us to dance the shuffle. We sold out long before our forties—probably in our early adolescence when we decided that others could determine how we should look, think, and act.

Many of us have so identified with male values that to ask who we are for ourselves is a conundrum.

We sold out because, much more than men, we have been socialized to conform. Both little boys and girls grow up in the woman-dominated world of home and school, where being "sugar and spice and everything nice" is rewarded. Little girls thrive; little boys, "the puppy-dogs' tails," receive no such payoff. If they are too compliant, they are considered sissies, and if they are aggressive and impulsive, they are "bad."

However, their characteristic adventurous behavior is an independent source of great pleasure, and is central to their developing sense of self. According to researchers Bardwick and Douvan, boys are motivated to develop inner-directed criteria of worth. Girls, on the other hand, remain pliant to the culture's demands because their behavior less often triggers cultural disapproval.

Given this situation, it is nothing short of amazing that some women eventually do question their role. But if being compliant ever had payoffs, at midlife they have fallen away. As one formerly quite traditional widow who took up jogging told me, "The old ways of behaving that my friends approve of weren't working for me. I decided I'd better be creative about my life."

But if we do not make this breakthrough, we are enmeshed in the youth fixation and victimized by our own self-hate. We also become estranged from one another, because the youth trip makes women rivals fighting for male attention rather than sisters valuing our worth. We've all felt it—at parties, in ladies' rooms—the way we check each other out. The generation gap is another effect of our self-hate. Older women envy younger women, younger women put down older women. This problem exists even in the women's movement.

Little White Lies

It's hard for us to go about the business of becoming ourselves because we are taught that there's no harm in being what we're not. We are taught to present ourselves in as good a light as possible—and for older women, this means a diffused light, preferably coming from the side: "I call it my confidence light," said Holly, an actress. "The first thing older actresses do is send their companion onto the stage, have all the lights put on, and then have the special lighting they need put in—side lighting. I won't go into a restaurant that has overheads."

We have been raised to be like chameleons. Film writer and director Joseph Mankiewicz made the following comment about Elizabeth Taylor, but it could apply to most of us to some extent:

Look, when you see Elizabeth now, you are seeing Mrs. John Warner, who is appearing on the stage under her maiden name, doing her husband no end of good and making him proud. Thus, she is successful in her primary role. Just as she was Mrs. Michael Wilding and had people in for English tea. Just as she was Mrs. Eddie Fisher and told Yiddish jokes and let him sing "That Wonderful Face" as she sat at a table night after night so the audience could see what he was singing about. Just as she was Mrs. Richard Burton and drank and fought like a Welsh broad. The principal role in Elizabeth's life has always been as the wife of the man she's married to.

She has been the same through all her marriages. She's been whatever she was supposed to be. Whatever the script called for, she played it.

We are everywhere encouraged not to worry about knowing who we are—or if we know, to lie and reap the advantages of lying. And the advantages are of course obvious, since being and looking over forty puts one at an obvious disadvantage in this society.

In a *Cosmo* article, Barbara Dahl tells us about the age-change game. Evidently many wives secretly collect Social Security checks at post office boxes rather than reveal their age to their husbands, and huge numbers of job applicants fudge their vital statistics on their résumés. It's also easy to get a new driver's license with a later birth date—and presto! the new, younger you, with a document to prove it.

Dahl gives us some other helpful hints for successfully turning back the clock, such as: ask a trusted friend how many years you can credibly lop off, learn to "think" your new age, remember what you're not supposed to remember, and teach your children to keep mum. Doctors should probably know the truth, but can be asked to keep it confidential. And since relatives often spill the beans, you are better off living far away. She concludes that the "age-change operation is almost without risk—a tiny ruse that hurts no one."

We lop off years, pounds, noses, sags. A tiny ruse that hurts no one? Ask Cinderella's sisters. "So the girl cut her toe off, squeezed her foot into the shoe, concealed the pain and went down to the prince." One pays a price, although the pain may even be concealed from ourselves.

Sara, a client of mine, came into therapy in order to deal with the pain of inauthentic living. At the start of our first session, she could only sob and sob. "What's the matter?" I asked. "The matter is *me*," she wailed. "I ruin everything! I'm tense all the time, my body aches, I feel completely false, numb, far from myself—I've learned *nothing*! I can't stand it anymore. *I want to be me*," she howled, beating her thighs with rage and pain.

There's something in us that hates our own self-hate—and our hatred of one another. Not being who we are ultimately is damaging to our self-esteem, as minorities who take enormous risks to affirm their identity know. But confronting the truth can only bring enormous relief and self-respect, in spite of the practical problems it may present. Women's desire to overcome their self-hate is powerful; it created the women's movement.

Authenticity and Time

Since authenticity is something we accomplish, it takes time—all the time we have. Time is the medium out of which we make ourselves. The past, present, and future are like the height, depth, and breadth of ourselves. We cannot be truly ourselves if we deny the flow of time; it is our dimensionality.

The answer to the question "Who am I?" must be answered in terms of past, present, and future. For me, an authentic relationship to my past means that I can say, yes, I remember Pearl Harbor, and the Lindy and the penny postcard. I stood on the back porch necking with my dates in mortal fear of discovery. I was in college during the McCarthy years, and we were not allowed to wear slacks even if it was the coldest part of winter. I remember when peaches tasted like peaches. And I remember Hitler and Hiroshima. I remember when there was no television. My friend Chellis grew up after the A-bomb and the small screen came along. She has never known a world with an assured future, without image makers, with peaches that taste like peaches. She is thirty-five and different from me.

My relationship to the present means that I can be fully in it. This is something that women are good at, but it is a strength that we often do not recognize. Our lives have called upon us to be responsive to what is happening moment to moment. We are masterful ad-libbers, improvisors, jugglers. As writer Marie Wells says, women's lives have been "enriched from childhood with a variety of colors, textures, rhythms and aromas far beyond the range of most men's day-to-day experiences. Their subtle attunement to the immediate environment adds further dimensions to their experiences of living at the center, of being centered, of being present, in the present."

To complete our answer to the question "Who am I?" we need also to consider the future. It is our sense of the future that makes us aware of our unlived living, unfelt feeling, undone deeds. Our desire for authenticity has momentum, it carries us forward; it pushes, presses, will not be stopped. Our sense of having time left allows us to wonder about who we could become. In her journal Katherine Mansfield wrote:

One heard, or thought one heard, the cry that began to echo in one's own being: "I have missed it. I have given up. This is not what I want. If this is all, then Life is not worth living."

But I *know* it is not all. How does one know that? Take the case of K.M. She has led, ever since she can remember, a very typically false life. Yes, through it all, there have been moments, instants, gleams, when she has felt the possibility of something quite other . . .

Our perspective on the future also leads us inevitably to a consideration of death. We become aware that we will eventually have to relinquish our hold on all we clutch at so avidly. Knowing this makes us less caught up in fears of taking risks or losing. The final outcome is already decided; the only question is how do we play the game between now and then.

Our authenticity, then, is our continuity through this past, this present, this future. We must bring our lives in harmony with the flow of time, instead of, like Alice, running desperately in order to always stay in the same place. Thus we liberate our energy for authentic living. However, the pressures upon women to freeze their lives at the "preferred" stages makes this a difficult task.

Most women I spoke to had difficulty living with the idea of continual change. For them, aging was not a ramp but a bumpy staircase. They would rest, say, at five-year landings, and then get reluctantly bumped upstairs into the next category. Women perceive themselves as not aging, and then suddenly aging quickly— *un coup de vieux*, as the French say. French cosmetologist Rose Godina commented: "A woman of thirty-seven will class herself in the 'young woman' category, until, say, forty or forty-five. A woman of fifty-nine thinks of herself as fifty-five, and a woman of fifty-three thinks of herself as fifty. And to the woman of seventy a woman of eighty is an 'old woman.' "

Models of Authentic Development

But as we look about us for models and maps to guide us toward authenticity, we find there is little available.

What falls most readily to hand is the male model of the quest or journey. This myth has been with us since the beginning of history under different names: Ulysses, Moses, Siddhartha. As the story goes, the hero receives the call and departs from his home (leaving behind wife and children). He sets out alone, undergoes ordeals which strengthen him and direct him toward his goal. The goal is the top of the mountain, and there he receives spiritual enlightenment and is transformed. He then returns home, master of both worlds.

The changes that women go through do not fit this linear model of the journey, and by its standards we fall short. But there are other models that serve us better.

The world of nature, not surprisingly, furnishes images which are more congruent with women's development. The living organism, after all, does not develop in linear fashion. It changes constantly, but each cell forever carries unchanging information about the whole that guides its development.

Janine Le Febvre, a Quebec educator, gave me a striking natural image. "Our birth is like a stone cast into a pond," she said. "Concentric circles form, growing ever wider. The outer circles owe their existence to the inner, and the core is never abandoned." We build on our original birthright as women.

Congruence

A hallmark of authenticity is personal congruence. Widening ripples make consistent shapes, the larger echoing the smaller. A congruent woman is consistent unto herself. Her physical appearance, gestures, and feelings match her words. As the psychologist Carl Rogers says:

> One of the things which offends us about radio and TV commercials is that it is often perfectly evident from the tone of voice that the announcer is "putting on," playing a role, saying something he doesn't feel. This is an example of incongruence. On the other hand, each of us knows individuals whom we somehow trust because we sense that they are being what they are, that we are dealing with the person him-

self, not with a polite or professional front. . . . Probably one of the reasons why most people respond to infants is that they are so completely genuine, integrated or congruent.

Congruence has the power of simple truth. We feel that we can relate immediately to congruent people. We sense that they are what they appear to be; we do not have to stop and "figure them out." On the other hand, we tend to be wary and cautious with incongruent people. We wonder what they really feel, who they really are. We wonder if *they* know. To be incongruent with respect to our age and experience means that we become a house divided against itself.

When I think of congruent women, the ones that first come to mind have *lived:* I think of Marcella, an inspiring Italian woman of sixty-five, who told me, "I've been rich, then poor, then interned as an anti-Fascist by the Italian government. It's completely different when you stand by your ideas. You choose your destiny and don't resent it—you go by your own feet and suffer much less. You do what's right and it gives you enormous strength." I think of my teacher Ida Rolf, who worked for forty years in obscurity because she was on to something, some new therapy. I think of Helen Caldicott, who decided that as a pediatrician she could not remain silent when the arms race threatened all life.

These women have in common a quality of transparency. They are willing to risk being who they are, to act on their convictions. They have little to hide, little to fear, because there is little that can be taken from them.

The Roar of the Kleenex

The concept of congruence has implications for women's development. Like the ripples that emanate from a pebble tossed into a pond, we will increase our range and power to the degree that we expand on who we are at the core.

Each one of us has to decide for herself of what this core consists. There are no right answers. But whether due to nature or nurture, there are some broad generalizations we can make about the central values in the lives of most women. This "core" is well illustrated by a story told to me by Jacqueline, a Frenchwoman:

> I was taking care of my nine-year-old nephew who was dying of cancer. He was sleeping in the adjoining bedroom. Suddenly, in the middle of the night, I woke up. At first I didn't know what had awakened me. Then I realized that I had been awakened by the sound of Jean-Michel's Kleenex as he tried to wipe his face where the cancer had eaten it away.

Jacqueline's attunement to her nephew's needs is not unusual for women. It is part of a constellation of qualities that could be roughly called "humanitarian concern."

These qualities are central to the functioning of any society, and women until now have primarily been the carriers for them. The care of the young, the old, the sick, the alienated, and the corresponding roles of mother, teacher, helper, and healer have traditionally been woman's bailiwick. They are also awarded very little status in our society.

Many researchers have identified the specific capacities which enable us to play these roles so well. Some of them are: the willingness to admit our vulnerability, sensitivity to the needs of others, the desire to enhance the quality of life for others, the recognition of the essential cooperative nature of existence, the ability to find self-worth and satisfaction in tasks that are not prestigious. Attunement, affiliation, and nurturing, in other words.

I am struck by the ubiquitousness of these concerns. A retired madam who missed her work told me:

> I was needed. I was helping people. I opened houses to protect women. Most of the ladies who worked for me were battered women; they were all in it for the money—to keep their children. I gave them refuge while they were bettering their lives. I taught them to act like ladies—to dress well, speak softly, not use bad language. We put in a hot line—a safety

phone number—for ladies out on call. But I only hired part-time people. It's too hard on the ladies to do it full time.

I learned constantly—it was a twenty-four-hour-a-day thing. I fixed banquets, learned how to entertain, to put Miss Right with Mr. Right, and so forth. There are three madams on the circuit that are over eighty years old, and I learned a lot from them.

And Mrs. Riley, an Irishwoman, told me:

I started nursing in London, as green as licks. My husband was in the service, and I got pregnant right away. When the child was born he only weighed three pounds. My mother had cancer of the eye. She went to the hospital to have it operated on, but she wouldn't stay the three or four weeks the doctors said. "There's a baby that needs me," she told them. She went right home to take care of my baby.

These core concerns have gotten a bad press lately, because they have usually been used to trap women. We need only think of the devoted, underpaid nurse whose doctor boss gets all the glory. Yet I'd like to speak up loud and clear in these pages for mother love, nurturing, and humanitarian concern in general. There is nothing wrong with our impulse to be of service. Quite the contrary. What is needed is a way to do so effectively and to have this recognized for the essential work it is.

The Ripple Effect

With age comes a widening of vision. The core remains, but the circles get larger and more inclusive:

I am more aware of the relationship of humans to each other. I express this through my work and there is a receptivity to it—maybe because I've learned to say things in a more acceptable way, maybe because of the danger the whole race is in.

There is a certain sense of the shrinking of time that is very difficult to accept. It impels me to do everything I can for the generations that are to come.

If we stopped in our need of becoming—either individually or collectively—we hit tragedy. Humanity is seeking to be more, just as individuals are seeking to be more.

These wider ripples are often more serene:

The process of aging is a great lightening up of false tensions that come from romance, from having certain ideas of yourself, and from things you think you have to have. It takes many years to become young. It is a slow process of undoing all the knots. And it takes courage to leave the security that youth, sex and the passport of attractiveness bring. But life is kind. It gives you time. Things happen slowly. You adjust. What you lose on one side you gain on the other.

The Midlife Paradox

Our core concerns often lead us into nurturing, healing, educating, and mediating kinds of work. But society frustrates our fullest expansion into these roles. These frustrations bring us to a paradox. We discover that to expand from our cores, we are going to have to become more than nurturers. We will need to add assertive, individualistic, confrontational skills to our emotional repertoire—skills that can move us out into the world. Once we are comfortable with this (hitherto male) vocabulary of risk-taking, winning and losing, we will be able to put some clout behind our concerns and devise ways to transcend unproductive frustration and conflict. The strength of our caring provides the motive power for us to overcome our fears about succeeding in a competitive world.

Mrs. Riley's story about her developing assertiveness is a perfect metaphor for this process:

My son's muscular dystrophy has changed my life. Wanting the best for him has driven me. The doctor said, "We have no magic wands. He'll be dead at seven. Take him home and when you get there, look at your daughters." And me standing there like a stewed prune listening to all of this! Can you imagine! I don't think I even noticed another person when I left that place.

But I would not take that for an answer. I took him to Lourdes when he was six. The priest said, "You'll never be able to carry that great boy all the way up that hill." But I said, "Never mind, father! I've come this far, I'm going all the way." So I just hoisted him on my shoulders and started climbing. Well, by the time we got to the third station of the cross, his runny nose started clearing up. He never had a clean nose before that. Then I put him down. Before long, he was running up the stations twice. After that his disease was dormant. He's eighteen now and has hardly any trouble.

Miracles may be too much to expect for most of us, but we surely have some hills to climb. "Wanting the best"—for *all* of us—drives us too.

I discovered this in Paris one spring afternoon. My fifteen-year-old daughter needed braces and I was combing the unfamiliar city looking for an orthodontist. I had started the day working on this book, which at the time I envisioned as one solely concerned with the *needs* of older women. Later that morning I had watched Carter and the Ayatollah Khomeini engage in mutual muscle flexing. From my vantage point in Paris, Afghanistan, Russia, and the United States all seemed much closer together— certainly within nuclear missile range. I suddenly realized that these male leaders were so caught up in their script that they could not be trusted to protect me, my family, or anyone else for that matter. I found myself wondering if Rina would live long enough to enjoy her straight teeth. At that moment it became clear to me that if I was to be a good mother, I would have to get my priorities straight. There was no point in worrying about crooked teeth and doing nothing about nuclear weapons.

And I also realized that my book would have to deal not only with our needs, but also with our *responsibilities.*

But it was not easy to make this shift, and in this I know I am not alone. "Going public" is wrenching for many of us.

We mostly live private lives, or on rare occasions we enter the public domain within male power structures. It absolutely boggles my mind what might happen if women would realize that the dirt in the rivers and oceans as well as the dirt on the kitchen floor is *our* dirt. What might the planet be like if all that intelligence, caring, endurance, and willingness to sacrifice could be extended from the private domain to a planetary consciousness! The hand that rocks the cradle could swing the balance to the side of survival (for there are only two sides now)—if only we could keep on thinking as women but translate it into political action. I mean by that of course a new kind of politics—not partisan but planetary. We can no longer wait to pick up the pieces after the damage is done. There will be no pieces to pick up unless we realize that to us as mature women all the children are our children now.

I am only one of the many who have felt the ripples widen and have stretched themselves proportionately.

But we have more stretching to do. Our world sickens from lack of nurturing care at every level of organization, from the local to the national to the global. Our most respected scientists predict the unthinkable, and the possibility of total catastrophe has become a fact of daily life. The sense of impending doom, whether from ecological disaster or nuclear holocaust, is always lurking around the edges of our consciousness.

The vacuum of mature feminine energy cries out to be filled. And yet such is our situation that we still say things like the following, from Terri Schulz's book *Bittersweet:*

> Almost every weekday afternoon I jump in my car and go to the local shopping center mall. I buy a bathtub mat, a coffee mug, some small thing. I don't have much money. But I buy

things to feel I exist. To select one item from among an array of things makes me feel I have taste, I can choose. I have some control over my life, I am still an individual.

Choosing a bathtub mat can only take us so far. What is really needed is a full range of opportunities to manifest what is inside, to engage in the process of trial and error, challenge and feedback that has largely been available only to men. Removing the barriers to these opportunities is therefore as necessary as our own work on ourselves. The study by the Lowenthal group found that the most gifted older women were also the most bitter and disappointed in their lives. This is understandable, as long as so many of us are still forced to the shopping mall in search of authenticity.

Right Action

Our vision of the importance of the personal—of each child, each living thing—is also the ultimate political vision for the nuclear age. Our humanitarian concern and our years of living have carved out a special role for us to play. We are the last generation that could wake up in the morning and take a breath without wondering what's in it. The last to nurse our babies without wondering what we were feeding them; the last to have taken the idea of a natural life span for granted. We therefore have a unique positive experience on which to build hope for the future. Our children need to see our hope and our righteous indignation, since many of them see only despair and are drowning in it. "We're not troubled by future shock," said Tish. "We've been shocked too much already."

Older women can no longer afford to remain the world's most underutilized resource. And as we begin to use the second half of our lives authentically, our youth hangup will lose its deathly grip on us.

We are highly motivated to make this shift for our own sakes. We have everything to gain and nothing to lose. But it is no longer possible to make a separation between helping ourselves and helping others. In fact, the very survival of human life may depend upon mature women laying claim to the power they have been denied.

We will, of course, need the cooperation of men, but they stand to gain as well. In the first place, men are also oppressed by our current system of gender arrangements. It's not just that they can't cry or play with their children enough. They—and we—live in a world made inhumane, routinized, and ultimately precarious by the double standard of sexuality and the double standard of aging.

By the year 1990, 36 million American women will be forty-five years old or older. We are no longer content to live on the dark side of the moon, and our vision will have an unprecedented numerical force behind it. Already our power is starting to be felt. For the first time in history, voting patterns of women, with respect to humanitarian concerns and world peace, are differing significantly from those of men.

There is no way at this juncture to promise a life of happiness to each one of us, if by happiness is meant gratification of our needs and desires. But the significance of our struggles can be promised. It is a privilege to be an older woman at such a historic moment.

Interview Questionnaire

1. Do you tell your real age? If not, when did you begin to conceal it?
2. Does your real age match your "inside feeling of your age"?
3. When is a woman no longer young?
4. Do you see your life as a continuum or divided into stages? How?
5. What has been the hardest/best/worst stage of your life?
6. What is this particular stage about?
7. When you were younger, could you imagine yourself at this age?
8. Can you imagine yourself older? What image do you have? How long do you expect to live?
9. Has your sense of time changed over the years?
10. How do you feel when you look in the mirror?
11. How much time/money do you spend caring for your body?
12. How do you feel about rejuvenating procedures like hair dye? Face lifts?
13. Talk about your health and your experience of menopause (or anticipation of this).
14. What role do sex and love play in your life?
15. How do you feel about solitude?
16. What role does work play in your life?
17. What are your fears? regrets? dreams? What is your advice to a daughter?
18. How do you feel about aging and dying? What have you experienced in those close to you, particularly your mother?
19. What else would you like to say that I have not thought to ask you?

Bibliography

Allen, Margaret. *Selling Dreams: Inside the Beauty Business*. New York: Simon & Schuster, 1981.

Baker, Ellsworth. *Man in the Trap: The Causes of Blocked Sexual Energy*. New York: Discus/Avon, 1967.

Barbach, Lonnie G. *For Yourself: The Fulfillment of Female Sexuality*. New York: Signet, 1975.

———— and Levine, Linda. *Shared Intimacies*. New York: Bantam/Doubleday, 1980.

Barrett, Michele, and Roberts, Helen. "Doctors and Their Patients: The Social Control of Middleaged Women in General Practice," in *Women, Sexuality and Social Control*, Carol and Bany Smart, eds. London: Routledge & Kegan Paul.

Bart, Pauline. "Depression in Middleaged Women," in *Woman in Sexist Society*, Vivian Gornick and Barbara Moran, eds. New American Library, 1972.

Bateson, Gregory. *Steps to an Ecology of Mind*. New York: Ballantine, 1972.

Berne, Eric. *Games People Play*. New York: Ballantine, 1964.

Block, Marilyn R.; Davidson, Janice L.; and Grambs, Jean D. *Women Over Forty*. Vol. 4, Focus On Women Series, Violet Franks, ed. New York: Springer, 1981.

Boston Women's Health Collective. *Our Bodies, Ourselves*. Rev. ed. New York: Simon & Schuster, 1976.

Broderick, Carlfred. "Sexuality and Aging: An Overview," in *Sexuality and Aging*, Robert L. Solnick, ed. University of California Press, 1978.

Broverman, Inge, et al. "Sex-Role Stereotypes: A Current Appraisal." *Journal of Social Issues*, 28 (1972), 59–78.

Brown, Judith K. "Cross-Cultural Perspectives on Middleaged Women." *Current Anthropology*, April 1982.

Bugenthal, James. *The Search for Existential Identity.* San Francisco: Jossey-Bass, 1976.

Butler, Mathilda, and Paisley, William. *Women and the Mass Media.* New York: Human Sciences Press, 1980.

Butler, Robert, M.D. *Why Survive?* New York: Harper Colophon, 1975.

Byrne, Eileen M., ed. *Women's Work, Men's Work: New Perspectives for Change.* Paris: UNESCO, August 14, 1980.

Carles, Emilie. *Une Soupe des herbes sauvages.* Paris: Jean-Claude Simeon, 1977.

Chernin, Kim. *The Obsession: Reflections on the Tyranny of Slenderness.* New York: Harper & Row, 1981.

Chesler, Phyllis. *About Men.* New York: Bantam, 1978.

———. *Women and Madness.* New York: Avon, 1972.

Clay, Vidal S. *Women, Menopause and Middle Age.* Pittsburgh: Know, Inc., 1979.

Cohen, Joan Z.; Levin, Karen; and Pealman, Joan. *Hitting Our Stride.* New York: Delacorte Press, 1980.

Colette. *Break of Day.* New York: Farrar, Straus & Giroux, 1961.

———. *The Vagabond.* New York: Ballantine, 1955, 1981.

———. *Gigi.* New York: Farrar, Straus & Giroux, 1952.

———. *Julie de Carneilhan.* New York: Farrar, Straus & Giroux, 1952.

———. *Chance Acquaintances.* New York: Farrar, Straus & Giroux, 1952.

Cornelison, Ann. *Women of the Shadows.* Boston: Atlantic/Little Brown, 1976.

Courtney, A., and Lockeretz, S. "A Woman's Place: An Analysis of the Roles Portrayed by Women in Magazine Advertisements." *Journal of Marketing Research,* 8 (February 1971), 92–95.

Cressanges, Jeanne. *La Vraie Vie des Femmes Commence d Quarante Ans.* Paris: Grasset, 1979.

Curlee, J. "Alcoholism and the Empty Nest." *Bulletin, Menninger Clinic,* 1969, 33: 165–171.

Curtis, Eugene H., M.D. *Aesthetic Surgery Trouble.* St. Louis: C. V. Mosby, 1978.

Daly, Mary. *Gyn/Ecology.* Boston: Beacon Press, 1978.

de Beauvoir, Simone. *All Said and Done.* New York: Warner Books, 1979.

———. *Force of Circumstance.* Vols. I and II. New York: Harper Colophon, 1964.

———. *Old Age.* New York: Penguin Books, 1972.

———. *The Second Sex.* New York: Vintage/Random House, 1974.

———. *The Woman Destroyed.* New York: Fontana/Collins, 1971.

Deutsch, Ronald. *The Key to Feminine Response in Marriage.* New York: Ballantine, 1968.

Dinnerstein, Dorothy. *The Mermaid and the Minotaur.* New York: Harper/Colophon, 1976.

Duncan, Isadora. *My Life.* New York: Liveright, 1955.

Dychtwald, Ken. "The Elder Within" and "Liberating Aging: An Interview with Maggie Kuhn." *New Age Journal,* February 1979, Vol. IV-8, 29–33 and 34–38.

Edgerton, Milton T., Jr., M.D., and Knorr, Norman J., M.D. "Motivational Patterns of People Seeking Plastic Surgery." *Plastic and Reconstructive Surgery,* 48, 6:551.

Ehrenreich, Barbara, and English, Deirdre. *Complaints and Disorders: The Sexual Politics of Sickness.* Old Westbury, N.Y.: Feminist Press, 1973.

———. *For Her Own Good: 150 Years of the Experts' Advice to Women.* Garden City, N.Y.: Anchor/Doubleday, 1979.

———. *Witches, Midwives and Nurses.* Old Westbury, N.Y.: Feminist Press, 1973.

Frazer, Sir James George. *The Golden Bough.* New York: Macmillan, 1950.

French, Marilyn. *The Women's Room.* New York: Summit, 1977.

Freud, Sigmund. *A General Introduction to Psychoanalysis.* New York: Permabooks, 1953.

———. *Outline of Psychoanalysis.* New York: W. W. Norton, 1949.

———. *New Introductory Lectures of Psychoanalysis.* New York: W. W. Norton, 1964.

———. "The Predisposition to Obsessional Neurosis." James Strachey, editor, *Collected Papers.* New York: Basic Books, 1959, 2, 130.

———. *Three Contributions to the Theory of Sex.* New York: Modern Library, 1938.

Friedan, Betty. *The Feminine Mystique.* New York: W. W. Norton, 1963.

———. *The Second Stage.* New York: Summit, 1981.

Frym, Gloria. *Second Stories.* San Francisco: Chronicle Books, 1979.

Fuchs, Estelle. *The Second Season.* Garden City, N.Y.: Anchor/Doubleday, 1978.

Gilligan, Carol. *A Different Voice.* Cambridge, Mass.: Harvard University Press, 1982.

Goin, John M., and Goin, Marcia K. *Changing the Body: Psychological Aspects of Plastic Surgery.* Baltimore: Williams & Wilkins, 1981.

Goin, Marcia; Goin, John; and Burgoyne, Rodney. "Face Lift: Patients'

Secret Motivations and Reactions to Informed Consent." *Plastic and Reconstructive Surgery*, Vol. 58–3 (1976), 273–279.

Goldwyn, M. D., ed. *The Unfavorable Result in Plastic Surgery*. New York: Little, Brown, 1972.

Gorer, Geoffrey. *Death Grief and Mourning*. New York: Doubleday, 1967.

Gornick, Vivian, and Moran, Barbara K., eds. *Woman in Sexist Society: Studies in Power and Powerlessness*. New York: Mentor, 1971.

Goulian, Dicran, and Curtiss, Eugene H., eds. *Symposium of the Aging Face*. Educational Foundation of the Association of Plastic and Reconstructive Surgery, Vol. 19, Denver, 1976.

Greer, Germaine. *The Female Eunuch*. New York: Granada/Paladin, 1971.

Griffin, John Howard. *Black Like Me*. Boston: Houghton Mifflin, 1977.

Griffin, Susan. *Woman and Nature*. New York: Harper/Colophon, 1978.

Grimm's Household Stories. New York: Mayflower Books, 1979.

Gross, Ronald; Gross, Beatrice; and Seidman, Sylvia. *The New Old: Struggling for Decent Aging*. Garden City, N.Y.: Anchor/Doubleday, 1978.

Guzzardi, Walter. "Demography's Good News for the 80s." *Fortune*, November 5, 1979.

Hamilton, Edith. *Mythology*. Boston: Little, Brown, 1942.

Harris, Louis, and associates. "Myths and Realities of Life for Older Americans," in *The New Old: Struggling for Decent Aging*, Gross, Gross, and Seidman, eds. Garden City, N.Y.: Anchor/Doubleday, 1978.

Heilbrun, Carolyn G. *Reinventing Womanhood*. New York: W. W. Norton, 1979.

———. *Toward a Recognition of Androgyny*. New York: Harper/Colophon, 1973.

Hemer, June, and Stanyer, Ann. *Handbook for Widows*. London: Virago, 1978.

Henley, Nancy M. *Body Politics*. Englewood Cliffs, N.J.: Spectrum/Prentice-Hall, 1977.

Hite, Shere. *The Hite Report*. New York: Dell, 1976.

Hollander, Nicole. *That Woman Must Be on Drugs*. New York: St. Martin's, 1981.

———. *Mercy It's the Revolution and I'm in My Bathrobe*. New York: St. Martin's, 1982.

Huyck, M. H., Eschen, C.; and Tabachnik, R. *Women's Attitudes Toward Radical Hysterectomy*. Chicago: Illinois Institute of Technology, 1973.

Jacobs, Ruth Harriet. *Life After Youth.* Boston: Beacon Press, 1979.
Janeway, Elizabeth. *Powers of the Weak.* New York: Morrow Quill Paperback, 1981.
Johnson, Don. *The Protean Body.* New York: Harper/Colophon, 1977.
Julty, Sam. *Men's Bodies, Men's Selves.* New York: Delta, 1979.
Kandel, Thelma. *What Women Earn.* New York: Linden Press/Simon and Schuster, 1981.
Kierkegaard, Soren. "The Sickness Unto Death," in *A Kierkegaard Anthology,* Robert Bretall, ed. Princeton, N.J.: Princeton University Press, 1946.
Kimmel, Douglas. *Adulthood and Aging.* New York: John Wiley & Sons, 1974.
Klein, Arnold, M.D.; Steinberg, James. H., M.D.; and Bernstein, Paul. *The Skin Book.* New York: Macmillan, 1980.
Kuhn, Maggie. *New Life for the Elderly.* Paper from Gray Panthers, 3700 Chestnut Street, Philadelphia, Pa. 19104, 1974.
LeClerc, Annie. *Parole de Femme.* Paris: Grasset, 1974.
Leduc, Violette. *La Bâtarde.* New York: Farrar, Straus & Giroux, 1965.
LeGuin, Ursula. "The Space Crone." *Co-Evolution Quarterly,* Summer 1976.
LeShan, Eda. *The Wonderful Crisis of Middle Age.* New York: Warner Books, 1973.
Levinson, Daniel J. *The Seasons of a Man's Life.* New York: Ballantine, 1978.
Lifton, Robert J. *The Broken Connection.* New York: Simon & Schuster, 1979.
———. *The Life of the Self.* New York: Simon & Schuster, 1976.
Linn, L. S., and Davis, M. S. "The Use of Psychotherapeutic Drugs by Middleaged Women." *Journal of Health and Social Behavior,* 12, December 1971.
Lloyd, Mollie. *The Change of Life.* Dublin: Arlen House, The Women's Press, 1979.
Lowenthal, Marjorie Fiske; Thurnber, Majda; and Chiriboga, David. *Four Stages of Life—A Comparative Study of Women and Men Facing Transitions.* San Francisco: Jossey-Bass, 1975.
Luce, Gay Gaer. *Your Second Life.* New York: Delacorte, 1979.
Lurie, Allison. *The War Between the Tates.* New York: Random House, 1974.
Maccoby, Eleanor Emmons, and Jacklin, Carol Nagy. *The Psychology of Sex Differences.* Stanford, Calif.: Stanford University Press, 1974.
Mander, Ani. *Blood Ties.* New York: Moon Books, Random House, 1976.

Mander, Jerry. *Four Arguments for the Elimination of Television.* New York: Morrow Quill Paperbacks, 1978.

Mann, W. Edward. *Orgone, Reich and Eros.* New York: Touchstone/Simon & Schuster, 1973.

Mansfield, Katherine. Diary excerpts in *Revelations,* Mary Jane Moffat and Charlotte Painter, eds. New York: Vintage, 1975.

Martel, Martin U. "Age-Sex Roles in American Magazine Fiction 1890–1955," in *Middle Age and Aging,* B. Neugarten, ed. University of Chicago Press, 1968.

Maslow, Abraham. *The Farther Reaches of Human Nature.* New York: Viking, 1971.

———. *Toward a Psychology of Being.* New York: Van Nostrand Reinhold, 1968.

Masters, William H., M.D., and Johnson, Virginia. *Human Sexual Response.* New York: Bantam, 1966.

Mathews, Andrew M.; Gelder, Michael G.; and Johnston, Derek W. *Agoraphobia: Nature & Treatment.* New York & London: Guilford Press, 1981.

Media Report to Women, 3306 Ross Place N.W., Washington, D.C. 2008.

Miller, Jean Baker, M.D. *Toward a New Psychology of Women.* Boston: Beacon Press, 1976.

Millet, Kate. *Sexual Politics.* New York: Doubleday, 1969.

Moffat, Mary Jane, and Painter, Charlotte, eds. *Revelations: Diaries of Women.* New York: Vintage, 1975.

Montagu, Ashley. *The Natural Superiority of Women.* New York: Collier Macmillan, 1974.

———. *Touching.* New York: Harper/Colophon, 1978.

Morgan, Robin, ed. *Sisterhood Is Powerful.* New York: Vintage, 1970.

Moss, Zoe. "It Hurts to Be Alive and Obsolete," in *Sisterhood is Powerful,* Robin Morgan, ed. New York: Vintage, 1970.

Munroe, Alice. "Dulse." *The New Yorker,* July 21, 1980.

Musgrave, Ross H., M.D. "Some Advice, Sage and Otherwise," *Plastic and Reconstructive Surgery,* 58, 3 (1976): 269.

Nellis, Muriel. *The Female Fix.* New York: Penguin, 1980.

Neugarten, Bernice, ed. *Middle Age and Aging.* University of Chicago Press, 1968.

No Longer Young: The Older Woman in America. Occasional Papers on Gerontology, No. 11. The Institute of Gerontology, Wayne State University, University of Michigan, 1974.

Oakley, Ann. *Sex, Gender & Society.* New York: Harper/Colophon, 1972.

Olsen, Tillie. *Silences*. New York: Delacorte Press, 1978.
———. *Tell Me a Riddle*. New York: Lippincott, 1961.
Orbach, Susie. *Fat Is a Feminist Issue*. New York: Berkeley Books, Paddington Press Ltd., 1978.
Pernitz, Katharine. *Beyond the Looking Glass*. New York: William Morrow, 1970.
Petty, David L. *An Analysis of Attitudes and Behavior of Young Adults Toward the Aged*. Palo Alto, Calif.: R. E. Research Associates Inc., 1979.
Prather, Jane, and Fiddell, Linda S. "Put Her Down and Drug Her Up: An Analysis of Sex Differences in Medical Advertising." Presented at the American Sociology Association Convention, August 1972.
Prime Time magazine, 420 W. 46th Street, New York, N.Y. 10036. "Well, You See, Your Mother Never Worked" by Diana Smith Yackel, March 1976, Vol IV, 2.
Rees, Thomas D. *Aesthetic Plastic Surgery*. Philadelphia: Saunders, 1980.
Reitz, Rosetta. *Menopause: A Positive Approach*. Radnor, Pa.: Chilton, 1977.
Riley, M., and Foner, A. *Aging and Society*. Vol. I: *An Inventory of Research Findings*. New York: Russell Sage Foundation, 1968.
Rogers, Carl. *On Becoming a Person*. Boston: Houghton Mifflin, 1961.
———. *On Personal Power*. New York: Delta, 1977.
Rogers, Natalie. *Emerging Woman*. Point Reyes, Calif.: Personal Press, 1980.
Rose, Louisa, ed. *The Menopause Book*. New York: Hawthorne, 1977.
Rosen, Marjorie. *Popcorn Venus*. New York: Avon, 1973.
Roszak, Betty, and Roszak, Theodore, eds. *Masculine/Feminine*. New York: Harper/Colophon, 1969.
Rubin, Lillian B. *Women of a Certain Age*. New York: Harper & Row, 1979.
Sarton, May. *Journal of a Solitude*. New York: W. W. Norton, 1973.
———. *Mrs. Stevens Hears the Mermaids Singing*. New York: W. W. Norton, 1965.
Scarf, Maggie. *Unfinished Business: Pressure Points in the Lives of Women*. Garden City, N.Y.: Doubleday, 1980.
Schulz, Terry. *Bittersweet*. New York: Penguin, 1976.
Scott-Maxwell, Florida. *The Measure of My Days*. New York: Penguin, 1968.
Seaman, Barbara, and Seaman, Gideon, M.D. *Women and the Crisis in Sex Hormones*. New York: Bantam, 1977.

Sheehy, Gail. *Passages: Predictable Crises of Adult Life.* New York: Bantam, 1976.

Shields, Laurie. *Displaced Homemakers.* New York: McGraw-Hill, 1981.

Singer, June. *Androgyny.* Garden City, N.Y.: Anchor/Doubleday, 1977.

Smith, Don. "The Social Content of Pornography." *Journal of Communication,* 26 (1976), 16–24.

Sontag, Susan. "The Double Standard of Aging." *Saturday Review of Literature,* September 1972.

Stimpson, Catharine R., and Person, Ethel Spector, eds. *Women, Sex and Sexuality.* University of Chicago Press, 1980.

Sullerot, Evelyn. *Woman, Society and Change.* New York: World University Library, McGraw-Hill, 1971.

Terkel, Studs. *Working.* New York: Avon, 1972.

Thorsen, Frances S. *Whither the Widow?* Master's thesis, Antioch University, San Francisco, 1981.

Tiger, Lionel, and Shepher, Joseph. *Women in the Kibbutz.* New York: Harcourt, Brace, 1976.

Toffler, Alvin. *Future Shock.* New York: Random House, 1970.

Tolson, Andrew. *The Limits of Masculinity.* New York: Harper/Colophon, 1977.

Trilling, Diana. *Mrs. Harris.* New York: Harcourt Brace Jovanovitch, 1981.

Tuchman, Gaye; Daniels, Arlene K.; and Benet, James. *Hearth and Home: Images of Women in the Mass Media.* New York: Oxford University Press, 1978.

Vaillant, George E. *Adaptation to Life.* Boston: Little, Brown, 1977.

von Franz, M. L. *The Feminine in Fairytales.* Irving, Texas: Spring Publications, University of Dallas, 1972.

Wass, Hannelae. *Dying: Facing the Facts.* New York: McGraw-Hill, 1979.

Weideger, Paula. *Menstruation and Menopause.* New York: Delta, 1975.

Weil, Simone. *Waiting for God.* New York: Harper/Colophon, 1951.

Wells, Marie. "What Women Have Learned Going Through Transitions." Presented to the United States Association for the Club of Rome Conference, March 16–18, 1980. Bethesda, Md.

Winter, Nina. *Interviews with the Muse.* New York: Moon Books, Random House, 1981.

Wylie, Philip. *A Generation of Vipers.* New York: Rinehart & Co., 1941.

ACKNOWLEDGMENTS

To the readers of the manuscript, particularly Ani Mander, Susan Griffin, and Nick Allen, I owe special thanks. Chellis Glendinning, Marilyn Kriegel, Michael Rustigan, Jerry Mander, Roz Parenti, Mora Rothenberg, Sam Julty, Don Johnson, Tillie Olsen, and Berne Weiss also read parts of it and gave me good feedback. Several physicians gave generously of their time, particularly Sadja Greenwood and Samuel Stegman. Drs. Stephen Mathes, Michael Taylor, and Luis Vasconez were also most helpful. Lillian Rubin, Tish Sommers, Tom Ucko, and Ken Dychtwald shared their perspectives about aging with me, and Diane Rabinowitz and Sara Alexander were typists/critics beyond the call of duty. I wish especially to thank my agent, Emilie Jacobson, and my editor, Joni Evans, who believed in the importance of what a new writer had to say and took a chance on me. Most of all, I owe a debt to all the women whom I interviewed. Many of them appear disguised in these pages, under fictitious names, but their enormous contribution made this book possible.

ABOUT THE AUTHOR

ELISSA MELAMED, PH.D., received her bachelor's and master's degrees from Radcliffe and Harvard and her doctorate in psychology from Columbia Pacific University. She has been an educational consultant and psychotherapist for the past twenty-five years. Dr. Melamed has three children and maintains a private practice in San Francisco.